The
Collector's Guide
—to—
New England

by Jerry and Suzanne Bowles
—Illustrated by Frank Sanford—

World Almanac Publications

New York, New York

Cover and interior design: Abigail Sturges.
Cover illustration and maps: Ralph Moseley.
Interior illustrations: Frank Sanford.

First published in

Distributed in the United States by Ballantine Books, a division of Random
House, Inc., and in Canada by Random House of Canada, Ltd.

Newspaper Enterprise Association ISBN No. 0-911818-46-4
Ballantine Books ISBN: 0-345-31503-0
Printed in the United States of America.
World Almanac Publications
Newspaper Enterprise Association, Inc.
A Scripps Howard Company
200 Park Avenue
New York, New York 10166

10 9 8 7 6 5 4 3 2 1

Contents

Introduction

There are a number of fine guides to New England on the market so you're to be forgiven, we suppose, if you wonder what's so special about this one. The answer is that this is--to the best of our knowledge--the first guidebook designed specifically for that intrepid breed of humankind know as the collector. A collector is the kind of person who will drive forty miles out of his way on an unpaved road just to look at a Townsend-Goddard cabinet or a Thomas Sheraton and eighty miles on ice for a chance to buy a bargain-priced Windsor chair in good condition. He or she is the kind of individual who enjoys history and treasures from the past and admires those who are dedicated to their preservation. From our experience in writing and editing for collectors over the years, we've tried to keep their particular interests in mind in assembling this book.

New England remains a collector's paradise; the greatest repository of Americana to be found. Named in 1614 by Captain John Smith, the six New England states--Connecticut, Maine, Massachusetts, New Hampshire, Rhode Island, and Vermont--have played a role in the history of the United States that is disproportionate to their sizes and populations. History is alive and well here and accessible to those with the taste and interest to seek it out. We hope you're that kind of person and that you enjoy the result of our labors. Good hunting!

Jerry & Suzanne Bowles
New York 1983

Connecticut

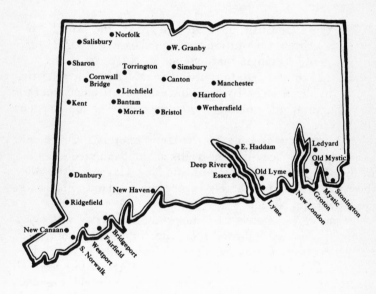

The "Constitution State"--in 1639, the world's first written constitution was signed here--is a 5,009 square mile rectangle that extends 90 miles east to west and 55 miles north to south. It is named for the river that neatly divides it in half which, in turn, got its name from the Algonquian word *quinnehtukqut*, meaning "beside the long tidal river."

Connecticut is a pleasant study in contrasts. On the one hand, there are heavily industrialized and populated cities like Bridgeport, Stratford, Hartford, and New Haven; on the other, there are wonderful, largely rural New England villages like Litchfield and Norfolk.

One of the state's first important industries was clock-making. This was followed soon after in the 19th centruy by the production of firearms. Samuel Colt built a factory here and the Colt .45 (as well as the Winchester rifle) are still made here. During the same period, Eli Whitney manufac-tured his revolutionary new cotton gin in New Haven and introduced the concept of standardized parts (an important element in mass production) at his firearms factory nearby. Connecticut still retains an important industrial base; particu-larly in electronics and high technology industries.

There are a lot of delights for the collector in Connecti-cut, ranging from the fabulous Mystic Seaport Museum in the south to the wonderful villages of Litchfield and Norfolk in the Berkshire foothills.

Bridgeport & Environs _____

Connecticut's second largest city (pop. 137,116), Bridgeport, has long been the state's manufacturing center. Elias Howe had his first sewing machine plant here; the American Gramophone Company (later the Columbia Phonograph Company) made the first records in Bridgeport. The city's leading citizen in the 19th century was Phineas T. Barnum, the circus magnate. Barnum served for a time as Bridgeport's mayor. One of his prize circus attractions, General Tom Thumb, a midget, was also a native of Bridgeport.

What to See

P.T. Barnum Museum, 820 Main Street. Located in an ornate Romanesque structure planned by Barnum himself, this unusual museum houses a splendid collection of circus memorabilia dating from the early days of the original Barnum & Bailey Circus. Don't miss the William R. Brinley Model Circus--500,000 hand-carved performers, animals, and circus equipment in miniature form. It took forty-two years to build. Open Tu-Sa 2-5. Adults $1; Children 50¢.

Museum of Art, Science and Industry, 4450 Park Avenue. The museum's elaborate collection of 19th century industrial products provides a kind of capsule history of this manufacturing city. There are exhibits where kids are encouraged to touch the displays, circus memorabilia, furnishings, and contemporary art with a scientific bent (like the mobile sculptures of Alexander Calder). The museum also has a good planetarium. Open Tu-Su 2-5, except Fr 10-5. Admission is $1 for adults; 50¢ for children, senior citizens, and students.

Bridgeport Environs. A few miles south of Bridgeport is the city of *Fairfield*, first settled in 1639. Its historic district includes seventy-five buildings dating from pre-Revolution to turn-of-the-century. Stop by the *Historical Museum*, 636 Old Post Road, and see its collection of paintings, glassware, lusterware, newspapers, and broadsides from the Colonial period. Open Mo-Fr 9:30-4:30; Su 1-5. Free.

This is also the home of the *Fairfield Historical Society* and if you ask they'll give you a small sheet directing you to the best sites in the historic district. Among them are the 1790

Town Hall and the *Village Green*. Located on the Green is the *Rising Sun Tavern*, built in 1780. Next door to the Historical Museum is the *Burr Mansion*, 739 Old Post Road, constructed in 1740 and then remodeled in Greek Revival style in the 19th century. Another must-see is the *Ogden House*, 1520 Bronson Road, an authentic saltbox farmhouse that features the traditional kitchen garden. Open mid-May to mid-October, Th, Su 1-4. Adults $1; children 50¢.

To the southwest of Bridgeport is *New Canaan*, a small, exclusive residential community settled in the first decade of the 18th century. The *New Canaan Historical Society*, 13 Oenoke Road, is a complex of building that includes the 1825 *Town House*, the archive of the society with a fine costume museum on the second floor; the *Cody Drugstore*, a re-creation of a mid-19th century apothecary shop; and an antique tool museum. Also located here is the *John Rogers Studio*, a home in the "Stick Style" which served as the studio of New Canaan sculptor John Rogers from 1877 to 1904. It displays some of his works as well as family furnishings. Open We, Th, Su 2-4. Adults $1.

To the north of Bridgeport is the city of *Ridgefield*, founded in 1708. The best site here is the *Keeler Tavern*, 132 Main Street. Built in 1772, the building was an inn until 1907 and a private residence until recently. It's also known as the "cannonball house" because it took fire from the British during the Revolution and a cannonball remains lodged in one of its walls. Handcrafts are on display and for sale in the tavern. Open year-round, We, Sa, Su 2-5 and by appointment. Adults $1.50; children 50¢.

Still further north is *Danbury*, settled in 1685 and incorporated in 1702. During the late 19th century, Danbury became the hat-making center of the New World.

The *Danbury Scott-Fanton Museum and Historical Society*, 43 Main Street, has three building open to the public. the *David Taylor House*, built in 1750, is a twin-chimney Colonial that now houses period furnishings, costumes, maps, and utensils. It's one of the few pre-Revolutionary homes spared the British torch because it was owned by a prominent Tory. The *Dodd* or *Barnum House*, 1770, is actually an early hat shop. *Huntington Hall* is a modern display building housing exhibits on science, art, and industry. Open We-Su 2-5. Donations accepted.

Where to Stay

West Lane Inn, 22 West Lane, Ridgefield, CT 06877. Tel: (203) 438-7323. Twenty rooms, all with baths. Doubles are $85 to $95 per night, including continental breakfast. Reservations should be made several weeks in advance. Owner: Maureen M. Mayer.

The West Lane is an historic Colonial building that was converted into an inn five years ago. The traditionally designed rooms also include all the modern conveniences, including--alas--color TV, air conditioning, and 24-hour telephone service. Some rooms have fireplaces and all have either one king-size bed or two queen size beads. Mobil's Travel Guide gives it four-stars. Only an hour and a quarter from New York City, this white frame mansion is in the heart of antique country and is near all the historic points of interest we've noted. Set on a broad green expanse of lawn, the Inn is a pleasant combination of old charm and modern convenience. No restaurant.

Where to Shop

Mrs. McGillicuddy's Shoppe, 82 King Street, Danbury, CT 06811. Tel: (203) 748-0041. Open Sa 10-5; Su 12-5; other times by appointment. Operated by Ruth and Jim Tibbetts for the benefit of the King Street United Church of Christ. In business for over seventeen years, featuring fine old clocks, china, glass, primitives, plated and sterling silver items, picture frames and framing; everything reasonably priced.

In New Canaan:

Jan and Larry Malis, PO Box 211, New Canaan, CT 06840. Tel: (203) 966-8510. Open by appointment. Jan and Larry Malis. This twenty-year-old shop sells antiquarian books and "ephemera of every description." Prices range from $1 to $10,000.

In Ridgefield:

Silver Spring Farm, Silver Spring Road, Ridgefield, CT 06877. Tel: (203) 438-7713. By appointment only. Judy Lenett. In business for more than fifteen years, this shop specializes in American folk art.

In South Norwalk:

Illustration House, Inc., 53 Water Street, South Norwalk, CT 06854. Tel: (203) 838-0486. Open by appointment. Walt or Roger Reed. Offers original art, illustrations previously published in magazines or books. Prices from under $100 to $10,000 and up.

In Westport:

Carpetbagger Antiques, 175 Post Road West, US 1, Westport, CT 06880. Tel: (203) 226-6429. Open daily 10-5. Michael J. Lundquist. This fifteen-year-old shop features country style furniture and accessories. Prices run from $10 to $5,000.

The Country Collector, Whippoorwill Lane, Westport, CT 06880. Tel: (203) 226-0591. By appointment only. William Gladstone. Specialist in American military photography, country antiques, decorator pieces. Prices range from $25 to $2,500.

Sunflower, 47 Riverside Avenue, Westport, CT 06880. Tel: (203) 227-3343. Open 11-4 Tu-Sa. Ann Laredo. Sunflower offers antiques, new baskets, decorative accessories, painted furniture, gifts. Prices run from $5 to $100.

Todburn Antiques, 243 Post Road West, Westport, CT 06880. Tel: (203) 226-3859. Open 10-6 Tu-Sa, also by appointment other times. G. G. Anderson II, Don W. Jobe. This shop, in business for over seventeen years, sells antique wicker, dolls, folk art, country furniture.

Ye Olde Lamp Shoppe, 315 Main Street, Westport, CT 06880. Tel: (203) 226-3104. Open 10-5 Tu-Sa. Bill Langton. Features antique lamps, hanging fixtures, wall lamps, reproduction shades and chimneys, miscellaneous brass and copper items. Most items are priced under $250.

Essex & Environs _____

Of all the Connecticut River towns with a maritime hertiage, Essex has retained most of that flavor. A shipbuilding center from 1720 until the mid-19th century, Essex today is a haven for yachts and pleasure craft. Its streets are still lined with Federal homes from the early years of the 19th century.

What to See

Connecticut River Foundation at Steamboat Dock. Located at the foot of Main Street, the Steamboat Dock was built in 1848 to service boats plying the river. A wooden warehouse, built in 1879, has been turned into a museum that houses a fine collection of maritime displays. Open all year; winter, Sa-Su 1-4; summer We-Su 1-5. Free.

Lt. William Pratt House, 20 West Avenue. Restored by the Essex Historical Society, the main building fronting West Avenue was built in 1740 but the original one-room building dates from the 17th century. It contains the Griswold Collection of Early American furnishings, has excellent period building details, and a nice herb garden out back. Open year-round, Tu-Th, Su 1-5. Adults $1.50.

Valley Railroad. A treat for railroad buffs, this authentic 19th century steam-powered locomotive chugs along the river valley to Deep River where you can connect with a river boat ride to Gillette Castle. The rides begin at Essex Junction just west of the Rte. 9 junction with Rte. 153. Open daily, May 9 to September 7; Tu-Th, Sa, Su from September 8 to November 1. Price for adults is $3.75-$7.75, children $2-$5, depending upon whether you also take the boat ride.

Old Lyme. Just a few miles south of Essex on the Connecticut River is the historic village of *Old Lyme*, today a peaceful relic of the past, its clapboard homes and tall white-spired Congregational Church a reminder of the great days of sail and the China Trade. For collectors, Old Lyme is delightful; one of the better preservation efforts in New England. Many of the remaining captains' homes are fine examples of Federal, Greek Revival, and Colonial styles. Best of the lot is the *Florence Griswold House*, 96 Lyme Street, an ornate Georgian mansion designed by Samuel Belcher and built in 1817. In 1900 Florence Griswold, daughter of the sea captain who bought it in 1841, turned it into an artists' retreat. Although the building is now inhabited by the Lyme Historical Society, the spirit of those artists remains in the dozens of paintings that hang on the walls (and, in fact, painted directly on the dining room walls). The home also has a splendid collection of Victorian dolls, dollhouses, toys, and children's books. Open year-round; summer, Tu-Sa 10-5, Su 1-5; winter We-Fr and Su 1-5.

Where to Stay

The Griswold Inn, 48 Main Street, Essex, CT 06426. Tel: (203) 767-0991. Twenty-two rooms, with baths. Doubles are $52, plus tax. Reservations should be made "well in advance" for weekends. Owner: William G. Winterer.

This historic Inn has been in business for 208 years! The main building was constructed in 1776 and was the first three-story structure in the state. "The Gris," as it is affectionately known, has four different--and splendid art collections. One is of steamboat prints by Currier & Ives and other important New York lithographers. It is considered to be one of the most important collections of its kind in America. Second, there is a collection of oil paintings by Antonio Jacobsen, an important marine painter from the turn-of-the-century. Third, there is a "library" of firearms--some fifty-five pieces that trace the development of the handgun and rifle from their origins in the 15th century. Finally, there is steamboat memorabilia--lots of it--a collection of artifacts ranging from ships' clocks and bells, to models, name boards, blocks and tackle...you name it. The collections are displayed throughout the public rooms of the Inn. There is a splendid restaurant serving fresh and genuine American country couisine. *New Yorker* once said of the Inn's Tap Room: "It just may be the best-looking drinking room anywhere in America." One of the best experiences for the collector. Highly recommended.

Where to Shop

In Deep River:

Jas. E. Elliott Antiques, Rte. 80, Winthrop Road, Deep River, CT 06417. Tel: (203) 526-9455. Open 11-5 Th-Sa or by appointment. James E. Elliott. This twenty-four-year-old shop offers British pottery and porcelain, specializing in Staffordshire. Also Empire and Regency furniture. Prices are from $50 up.

Winthrop Corners Antiques, Rte. 80, Winthrop Road, Deep River, CT 06417. Tel: (203) 526-9462. Open daily 12:30-5:30. William B. Gottlieb. In business for more than twenty years, sells out-of-print books and a small selection of

English and Continental furniture prior to 1830. Books are priced up to $250, antiques up to $3,500.

Jim Miller Antiques, Town Street, Rte. 82, East Haddam, CT 06423. Tel: (203) 873-8286. Open weekends and odd hours. Gerry Miller. More than thirty-five years in business, Miller offers unique and unusual pieces, American Indian, African, antiquities, art deco, early American hanging fixtures, architectural items. (2 miles from Goodspeed Opera House.)

In Essex:

E.J. Danos and Co. - Sports Art, One Essex Square, Essex, CT 06426. Tel: (203) 767-0528. Open daily 10-6. Joe Danos. This shop features antique duck decoys, 18th century antiques. Prices run from $40 to $30,000.

Forefather's Shop Antiques, Saybrook Road at South Main Street, Essex, CT 06426. Tel: (203) 767-8962. Open by chance or by appointment. Marian V. Dock. Sells country type furniture and accessories. Prices range from $5 to $3,000.

Francis Bealey American Arts, 3 South Main Street, Essex, CT 06426. Tel: (203) 767-0220. Open 11-4 Mo-Sa. Francis Bealey. Features period American furniture, American paintings of the 19th and early 20th centuries, related decorative arts. Prices run from $35 to $75,000.

Robert Spencer, River Road, Essex, CT 06426. Tel: (203) 767-8655. Open by appointment. Robert Spencer. This twenty-six-year-old shop specializes in American and English furniture, paintings, porcelain, silver of the 18th century. Prices start at $100.

Valley Farm Antiques, Saybrook Road, Rte. 154, Essex, CT 06426. Tel: (203) 767-8555. Open daily 10-4. Ellsworth E. Stevison. In business for over twenty-four years, Valley Farm offers furniture, guns, paintings, glass, china, American Indian, Eskimo, and African artifacts. Prices range from $1 to $18,000.

In Lyme:

Clocks, Rte. 156, Box 194, Lyme, Ct 06371. Tel: (203) 434-1052. Open daily 8-5. Charles M. Murphy. This shop specializes in antique and old clocks of New England origin. Also repairs early clocks. Prices are from $100 to $20,000.

In Old Lyme:

Antiques Associates of Old Lyme, 83 Halls Road, Box 882, Old Lyme, Ct 06371. Tel: (203) 434-2001. Open daily 11-5. A diverse selection of quality antiques: pottery and porcelain, American and English furniture, quilts, majolica, floblue, prints, oriental mugs, orientalia, objets de vertu.

Falcons Roost Antiques and Appraisals, 2 Four Mile River Road, Old Lyme, Ct 06371. Tel: (203) 739-5879. Open by chance or by appointment. Marilyn and Ed Bierylo. In business for more than twenty-five years, the Bieryloes offer American country furniture and accessories.

Hartford & Environs _____

Walking among the glistening modern office towers of downtown Hartford, it is hard to believe this is a city founded before the reign of Louis XIV. Settled by Puritans from the Massachusetts Bay Colony in 1635, it later became a center for trade, agriculture, manufacturing, and--in this century--insurance. The Fundamental Orders of Connecticut, the governing document drawn up by members of the Hartford Colony in 1639, is regarded by many historians as the world's first constitution. This historic town has also been home to such great writers as Harriet Beecher Stowe, Mark Twain, and the modern poet Wallace Stevens who was, interestingly enough, also an insurance executive.

What to See

Old Statehouse, 800 Main Street. Built between 1793 and 1796, this three-story brick and brownstone structure is America's oldest statehouse and one of the nation's most historic sites. In addition to being the first public building designed by the famed Boston architect Charles Bulfinch, it was also the venue of the Hartford Convention of 1814, which declared New England's opposition to the War of 1812, and it was host to General Lafayette, who visited the city in 1824. The building served as the State Capitol until 1879 and then as Hartford's City Hall until 1915. Gilbert Stuart's most famous portrait of George Washington is on permanent display here.

Open year-round, Mo-Sa 10-5. Admission is 50¢ for adults; 10¢ for children.

Connecticut State Capitol, Capitol Avenue. This Gothic Revival building of marble and granite, constructed in 1872, sports an impressive gold dome, towers, turrets, and moody statues of eminent native sons. Historic memorabilia on display includes a bronze statue of Revolutionary War hero Nathan Hale, battle flags of the state's Civil War regiments, and a replica of the Liberty Bell. Guided tours are available. Open year-round, Mo-Fr 9-3:30. Free.

Wadsworth Atheneum, 600 Main Street. One of New England's better museums, although relatively unknown, the Atheneum was founded in 1841 by Daniel Wadsworth as the first public art gallery in the nation. Hartford native J.P. Morgan donated many Greek and Roman bronzes in 1917. The museum's collections run the gamut: paintings by early Dutch, Italian, and Spanish masters; extensive collections American and British silver; a comprehensive gathering of Meissen porcelain; a fine collection of firearms donated by Colt; and many modern paintings. Most controversial of the Atheneum's possession is a contemporary sculpture by Carl Andre called *Thirty-Six Boulders*. It is precisely what the title says it is and costs a mere $87,000. Open all year, Tu-We-Fr 11-3; Th 11-8; Sa-Su 11-5. $2 for adults; $1 for children.

Museum of Connecticut History, 231 Capitol Avenue. History buffs will want to peek into this museum for a look at the Royal Charter of 1662. This is the document that was supposedly hidden inside an oak tree to keep it from falling into the hands of an agent of King James II, who wanted to revoke it in 1687. Other items of interest include a collection of Colt firearms and old Connecticut clocks. Open year-round Mo-Fr 9-5; Sa 9-1.

First Church of Christ (Center Church), Gold and Main Street. Site of the state's ratification of the Constitution, the Ancient Burying Ground here is believed to be the grave-site of Rev. Thomas Hooker, founder of Hartford. Open all year, daily 1-4.

Amos Bull House, 59 Prospect Street. Built in 1788, this is one of several historic homes in the downtown area. Many of the windows, dormers, and much of the brick work are believed to be original. Open year round, Mo-Fr 8:30-4:30.

Butler-McCook Homestead, 396 Main Street. Built in 1782, this landmark house is the current home of the Antiquarian and Landmark Societies. Many of the Butler family's original possessions are on display. A carriage house in back contains old bicycles, sporting equipment, and uniforms. Open daily from May 15 to October 15 12-4; October 16 to May 14 Tu-Th-Sa-Su 12-4. Admission is $1 for adults; 25¢ for children.

Western Hartford. This section of town was home to several famous artists and writers. Most revered among them is Mark Twain, who lived in one of a cluster of fine Victorian dwellings that stood on Nook Farm. The *Mark Twain House*, 351 Farmington Ave, was Twain's home from 1874 until the early 1890s. Both *The Adventures of Tom Sawyer* and *The Adventures of Huckleberry Finn* were written in this fancifully-designed house which combines Queen Anne, Victorian, and Mississippi steamboat styles. Just next door is the home of *Harriet Beecher Stowe*. Less grand than the Twain house, this two and a half story brick cottage contains many of the original furnishings, including the table on which parts of *Uncle Tom's Cabin* were written. Both houses are open year round, September 1 to May 31, Tu-Sa 9:30-4, Su 1-4; June-August daily 10-4:30. Combination tickets cost $3.50 for adults; $1.75

for children. While you're in the neighborhood, pay a visit to the *Connecticut Historical Society*, 1 Elizabeth Street. Artifacts on display include memorabilia from local history and an extensive collection of Colonial and Federal period furniture. Open all year, Mo-Fr 1-5.

Hartford Environs. Several town in the immediate Hartford area are worth a visit for the historic homes that can be seen. In Manchester, there is the *Cheney Homestead*, 106 Hartford Road, built by Timothy Cheney in 1780. Cheney was the founder of the nation's first successful silk mill and he and his descendants established one of the largest silk mill communities in the New World. The white frame house contains many family antiques and the mansions of other family members can be found at 20, 21 and 48 Hartford Road. The *Cheney Historic District* includes the Cheney mansions, several churches and schools, over 200 millworkers' houses, and about twenty-four mill buildings dating from the 18th and 19th centuries. Open all year, Th, Su 1-5. 50¢ for adults.

In Bristol, there are two main attractions. One is the *American Clock and Watch Museum*, 100 Maple Street. The major part of the museum is housed in the Miles Lewis House (1801) and it features many clocks manufactured in Bristol in the mid-19th centruy as well as the accounting desk of Eli Terry, Jr., a famed clockmaker. The museum has one of the largest clock collections in the nation. Open April 1 to October 31, daily 11-5. Adults $2.50; $1.25 for children. The other Bristol attraction is the *Lake Compounce Carousel*, Lake Avenue in the Lake Compounce Amusement Park, which is one of the country's oldest fair grounds. The carousel has a turn-of-the-century Wurlitzer organ and sixteen rows of horses. Open weekends from Easter to mid-June; daily from mid-June to Labor Day. Parking is $1.

The *Westersfield Historic District* is one of the state's best. The community has its roots in the shipbuilding and trade that flourished along the Connecticut River in the 19th century and the district features numerous attractive and historic homes, most of them still privately owned. Among the public landmarks are the *Capt. James Francis House*, 120 Harford Avenue. It dates from 1793 and remained in the family for 170 years. The furnishings reflect the entire period of their occupancy. Open June 15-October 15, Sa 1-4, Su 12-4. Adults

75¢; children 25¢. The *Isaac Steven House* on Main Street dates from 1788 and also includes the furnishing of generations of occupants. Open year round, Tu-Sa 10-4; Su 1-4 between May 15 and October 15. Admission is $1.50 but this also gets you into the *Joseph Webb House*, 211 Main Street, and the *Silas Deane House*, 203 Main Street. The Webb house was the site of a meeting between George Washington and the French General Count de Rochambeau. The historic meetings, which lasted for several days and probably took place in the south parlor, resulted in an alliance with the French that led to Cornwallis's defeat at Yorktown. In addition to being a home where "George Washington slept," it features some fine old Connecticut cabinetry and silver work. The Deane House was built in 1764 and belonged to a delegate to the First Continental Congress. In 1776, he was sent to France to develop trade and subsequently fell into disfavor with Congress. He never returned home and supposedly lived ever-after under the cloud of scandal for alleged wrong-doing while abroad. All of the house's furnishings date from before 1775. The well-appointed house is said to have been visited by both Washington and John Adams. Same hours and admission charge as the Webb and Stevens Houses.

Where to Shop

In Bristol:
Dick's Antiques, 670 Lake Avenue, Bristol, CT 06010. Tel: (203) 584-2566. Open 10-4, Mo-Fr. Richard Blaschke. In business more than twenty-two years, Dick's offers oaks, walnut, mahogany, wicker and Victorian furniture; also carries a complete line of curved cabinet glass for china closets. Prices range from $10 to $10,000.

Ole' Lamplighter Antiques, 200 Wolcott Road, Bristol, CT 06010. Tel: (203) 583-5395. Open 1-5 daily or by appointment. Rita Semprini. This twenty-five-year-old shop sells Victorian lighting, general merchandise. Priced "to suit everyone's pocketbook."

In Canton:
1784 House Antiques, Rte. 44, On the Green, Canton, CT 06019. Tel: (203) 693-2622. Open daily 10-5. Myrtle

Colley. Over twenty-five years in business. Specializes in Chinese export, jade, ivories, Tiffany, Galle, Lalique, Orientals, period furniture, Meissen, and so forth. Prices from $100 up.

The Cob-Web Shop and Flea Market, Junction Rtes. 44, 202, 179, Canton, CT 06019. Tel: (203) 693-2658. Open weekends or by chance. Dolly Rudder. This fifteen-year-old shop offers all kinds of collectibles.

The Frame Up, 162 Albany Turnpike, Rte. 44, Canton, CT 06019. Tel: (203) 693-6148. Open 10-5:30, Mo, We-Sa. In business for sixteen years, The Frame Up specializes in antique frames, also custom framing; old prints, country, Victorian. Prices range from 50¢ to $250.

In Hartford:

Shirley Gold, Books and Ephemera, 56 Coolidge Street, Hartford, CT 06106. Tel: (203) 525-9639. Open daily 9-6. Shirley Gold. In business over fifteen years. Rare, used, and out-of-print books, letters, documents, trade cards, prints, paper, collectibles, Americana. Near the Wadsworth Atheneum. Prices run from $5 to $5,000.

The Unique Antique, Civic Center Shops, Hartford, CT 06103. Tel: (203) 522-9094. Open 10-9 Mo-Fr, 9-6 Sa. Antique jewelry, glassware, silver, any "distinctive item."

In Manchester:

Trader World Antiques, 397 Tolland Turnpike, Manchester, CT 06040. Tel: (203) 646-9288. Open daily 10-4. This cooperative of seven dealers features furniture, glass, pottery, frames, paper goods. Moderate price range.

In Simsbury:

C. Russell Noyes, 9 Hopmeadow Street, Simsbury, CT 06070. Tel: (203) 658-5319. Open 9-5 daily. In business thirty years. Furniture of 18th and early 19th century; copper, woodenware, tin, small accessories. Prices range from $10 to $3,000.

Foster and Lanergan Antiques, 56 County Road, Simsbury, CT 06070. Tel: (203) 658-9841. Open by appointment. Lawrence A. Foster. Specializes in country Americana. Prices run from $10 to $10,000.

In West Granby:

Shirley E. Fantone Antiques, 175 Simsbury Road, West Granby, CT 06090. Tel: (203) 653-6411. Open daily 10-5. Shirley E. Fantone. This shop, in business over thirty years, sells a general line: glass, china, copper, brass, toleware, woodenware, furniture, clocks.

Litchfield & Environs

Litchfield is one of those villages that time forgot with the happy result that it is among the most picturesque of New England townships. Named for Litchfield, in Staffordshire, England, the village was settled in 1719 by settlers from Hartford and Windsor. Their early town planning persists to this day in the broad green and quiet side streets. Ethan Allen was born here. So was Henry Ward Beecher. Judge Tapping Reeve started the first law school in the nation in Litchfield. Litchfield, and the nearby villages of Norfolk, Bantam, Cornwall Bridge, Kent, Salisbury, Sharon, Morris, and the city of Torrington, make up the antiques center of Connecticut.

What to See

Litchfield Historic District. The entire center of the village is included in this district which is also a National Historic Landmark. For a flavor of how life was lived in Colonial times, all you need do is walk through this district which is occupied by Litchfield citizens today. Among the buildings to see are *Sheldon's Tavern*, built in 1760, on North Street and the nearby *Julius Deming House*, a 1793 Georgian mansion designed by William Spratt (who also remodeled the tavern). Spratt was an officer in the British Army who was taken prisoner during the Revolutionary War and then became a local architect of some note. One of the village's earliest houses is the *Oliver Wolcott, Sr. House* on South Street, built in 1753. Wolcott was a state senator, governor, delegate to the Continental Congress, and signer of the Declaration of Independence. Just across the street is the *Tapping Reeve House*, built in 1773. It includes a one-room school that was the nation's first law school. Graduates of this cabin academy included

Aaron Burr, John C. Calhoun, three Supreme Court justices, ninety Congressmen, and twenty-six Senators. Alas, no Presidents. The schoolhouse and Judge Reeve's home are open May 15 to October 15, Tu-Sa 11-5. Adults $1.50; children 50¢.

Another happily overlooked community to the north is *Norfolk*, settled in 1738 and incorporated twenty years later. Maple sugar was big here during the 19th century but the village's reputation as a summer resort today is due mainly to a rich patriarch named Joseph Batell, whose sons Joseph, Jr. and Robbins became patrons of the arts. It was Robbins who brought music concerts to this small town in the Berkshire foothills. The elder Batell's home *Whitehouse*, a mansion built in 1799, is now the headquarters of the Yale Summer School of Music and Art. On the eastern edge of the Village Green is the *Historical Society Museum*, which has displays of decorative arts, costumes, folklore, maps, and historical artifacts. Open June 16 to September 14, Sa 10-12, 2-5 and Su 2-5. On the south side of the Green is a fountain designed by Stanford White.

With a population of around 40,000, *Torrington* is the largest city in this part of Connecticut and also its industrial center. The first settler arrived in 1738. In the mid-19th century the city was known for its brass products. Its most famous native son is John Brown, the abolitionist. See the *Torrington Historical Society*, 192 Main Street. It's housed in a late-Victorian structure known as the *Hotchkill-Fyler House*, built in 1890. Many original furnishings are on display and there are exhibits covering the social and industrial history of the town from 1750 to present. Open all year, Mo-Fr 8-4. Also, see the *Turner Museum*, Torrington Library, 12 Daycoeton Place, which exhibits items of local history, antique glass, and dolls.

Where to Stay

Mountain View Inn, Rte. 272, Norfolk, CT 06058. Tel: (203) 542-5595. Eleven rooms, five with private bath. Doubles run $52-$57, including breakfast. The Inn's restaurant features continental cuisine. Reservations should be made one month in advance. Innkeepers: Connie and Tom Mazol.

The Mountain View is located in an 1875 Victorian mansion overlooking the historic village of Norfolk. Each guest room is individually decorated with antiques and several have large, four-poster beds. The Inn is in the heart of antiques country. There's a weekly auction in Norfolk. many antique shops, and two other auction galleries in neighboring villages. Open year-round. Great for cross-country skiing outings in winter; the Yale music concerts in summer.

Where to Shop

In Bantam:

Gooseboro Brook Antiques, Old Turnpike Road off US Rte. 202, Bantam, CT 06750. Tel: (203) 567-5245. Open by chance or by appointment; open most weekends. Carolyn Phelps Butts. Gooseboro Brook sells country antiques, furniture and accessories, some glass, silver, deco and art nouveau. Prices from $5 to $3,000 and up.

In Cornwall Bridge:

The Brass Bugle, Rte. 45, Cornwall Bridge, CT 06754. Tel: (203) 672-6535. Open daily 8-5. Louise and Robert Graham. In business for more than twenty years. Furniture, china, glass, dolls, primitives, vintage clothing, fabrics, quilts, and so forth. 18th century barn.

G.K. Holmes, Antiques, Rtes. 7 and 45, Cornwall Bridge, CT 06754. Tel: (203) 672-6427. Open daily 8-8. Gunnar K. Holmes. This thirty-year-old shop offers American antiques, furniture, accessories, toys, and dolls. Prices from $10 to $3,500.

Harry Holmes Antiques, Rte. 7 and Carter Road, Cornwall Bridge, Ct 06754. Tel: (203) 927-3420. Open daily 8-5. Harry Holmes. In business more than forty-three years, Harry Holmes specializes in antique furniture, clocks, and accessories. Prices range from $1 to $2,000.

In Kent:

Bull's Bridge, Rte. 7, Kent, CT 06757. Tel: (203) 927-3448. Open daily 11-5. Stephen Fellerman. Hot glass studio and gallery featuring work by the owner. Prices from $12 to $500.

Olde Station Interiors and Antiques, Main Street, Rte. 7, Kent, CT 06757. Tel: (203) 927-4493. Open Tu-Sa 10-5; Su

11-5; closed Mo or by appointment. Eugene D. Stillwaggon. Olde Station sells English and French antiques, unique lamps, reproduction furniture, art, and accessories; interior design. Prices run from $15 to $20,000.

In Litchfield:

Harry W. Strouse Antiques, Maple Street, Litchfield, CT 06759. Tel: (203) 567-0656. Open by appointment. Harry Strouse. In business for more than thirty years, Harry W. Strouse offers silver, glass, china, tools, books, paintings, rugs, furniture, prints, folk art, and so forth. Prices range from $1 to $1,000.

Litchfield Hill Antiques, On the Green, Litchfield, CT 06759. Tel: (203) 567-8607. Open 10-5:30 We-Sa, 12-5 Su. Clarence W. Pico, John A. Wright. Features 18th and 19th century furniture and decorations; Orientalia, country and formal, with emphasis on American and English formal. Prices from $10 to $5,000, generally $100 to $2,000.

Thomas D. and Constance R. Williams, Brush Hill Road, Litchfield, CT 06759. Tel: (203) 567-8794. Open by appointment only. Constance R. Williams. This forty-year-old shop offers 18th and 19th century American decorative arts, specializing in antique American pewter. Prices run from $65 to $25,000.

Thomas McBride Antiques, South Street, Litchfield, CT 06759. Tel: (203) 567-5476. Open 9-5 Mo-Fr. Thomas McBride. In business for fifteen years, this shop features glass, silver, china, furniture. Prices range from 50¢ to $12,000.

In Morris:

Lake Forest Art and Antiques, Rte. 209, Morris, CT 06763. Tel: (203) 567-8563. Richard Van Nesse. Marble, bronze sculpture, paintings, furniture, also country items. Prices run from $5 to $100,000.

T' Other House Antiques, Rte. 63, Litchfield Road, Morris, CT 06763. Tel: (203) 567-9283. Open by appointment or by chance. Margaret E. Gardiner. In business for more than twenty-five years, this shop offers a general line.

In Salisbury:

Undermountain Weavers, Undermountain Road, Salisbury, CT 06068. Tel: (203) 435-2321. Open 10-6 generally, but phone first. Eric H. Gerstel. Undermountain Weavers specializes in handwoven woolen and cashmere fabrics and garments made from these. Prices run from $10 to $500.

In Sharon:

Sharon Antiques Ltd., Cornwall Bridge Road, Sharon, CT 06069. Tel: (203) 364-5707. Open by appointment. Walter H. Rick. This sixty-nine-year-old shop specializes in antique clocks, silver, the unusual in decorative accessories.

In Torrington:

Arthur Shaw Antiques, 206 New Litchfield Street, Torrington, CT 06790. Tel: (203) 482-7200. Open Mo-Sa 10-5, closed Su. Arthur Shaw. In business more than eighteen years, Authur Shaw sells "everything." Prices range from $2 to $20,000.

Barredo's Antiques and Used Furniture, 2496 South Main Street, Torrington, CT 06790. Tel: (203) 482-0627. Open 10-5:30 Tu-Sa. Oak and Victorian furniture, glassware, jewelry, used furniture, and so on. Prices from $1 to $3,000.

Mystic, Stonington, New London, & Groton

Located on the Mystic River, the picturesque village of Mystic is one of New England's most delightful tourist destinations. An old maritime community of white clapboard houses and warehouses, Mystic has been turning out boats since the 17th century. A center of the China Trade in the early 19th century, the village later became a whaling port whose fleet numbered eighteen vessels. Mystic today is known mainly for the Mystic Seaport, a museum village that recreates the atmosphere of earlier days when the sea was the center of commerce for all the towns along this coast.

What to See

Mystic Seaport Museum, Greenmanville Avenue. The seaport stands on a seventeen-acre tract that was once the Greenman shipyards. Its collection now includes more than seventy buildings and 200 ships, plus a working shipyard and 19th century general store. There is also a children's museum, a planetarium, and many delightful exhibits. The Seaport's major attraction is the whaling ship *Charles W. Morgan*. The wooden ship dates from 1841 and was in service until 1921. It is now a National Historic Landmark. From May to October, you can board the Seaport's resident steamboat, the *Sabino*, for a cruise up the Mystic River. Built in Maine in 1908, the *Sabino* is the last of the coal-fired passenger steamboats. Near the *Sabino*'s berth is the *Henry B. DuPont Preservation Shipyard*, where you can watch ship repair and preservation work being done and wander among various interesting buildings.

Many of the Seaport's structures are quite unique. The *Shipsmith Shop*, for example, was transported here from its original site in New Bedford and it is the only example of a 19th century marine smith shop known to exist. It's still used to make the ironware needed to restore the Seaport's fleet. The *Mystic Bank*, constructed in 1833, was moved from Old Mystic town to the museum in 1948. All of the granite two-story Greek Revival structure is original, except for the front portico. Other interesting stops are the *Shipcarver's Shop*, which displays such haunting naval artifacts as figureheads, eagles, and other antique carvings, and the *Mystic Press*, an exhibit re-creating a 19th century print shop. In total, the Seaport has fourteen wharves and piers, many cobblestone paths, and numerous homes open for touring, in addition to its large fleet. The Seaport is open daily (except Christmas) March to November 9-5; December to March 9-4. From May to September, the grounds are open daily until 8. Admission is $7.50 for adults; $3.75 for children.

Although there are two historic districts in Mystic (The *Mystic Bridge Historic District* on the east side of the Mystic River and the *Mystic River Historic District* on the west), the best home to see is in neither. The *Denison Homestead*, or Pequotsepos Manor, is located on Pequotsepos Avenue. A two-story shingled landmark, this house was built in 1717 and remained in the same family until 1941. Eleven generations of family possessions are exhibited, with each room of the house reflecting a different era. Operated by the Denison Society, the home is open from May 15 to October 15, Tu-Su 1-5. Admission is $1.25 for adults; 50¢ for children.

The nearby village of *Stonington* was an important fishing and whaling port in the 19th century. Sometimes overlooked by visitors to the Mystic Seaport Museum, this pleasant village has more than its share of delights. The *Stonington Historic District* comprises some 450 Federal, Greek Revival and shingle-style homes, only 63 of which were built in this century. The houses range from the humble *Thomas Ash House*, 5 Main Street, circa 1780, to the lavish *Ira Palmer House*, 53 Main Street, built in 1847. It combines Greek Revival with some Italiante flouishes. Another splendid example of Greek Revival is the *Peleg Hancox House*, 33 Main Street, built in 1820. All of these homes are still in private hands but can be viewed from the street.

Whitehall Mansion, located on Rte. 26, is a gambrel-roofed home restored by the Stonington Historical Society. It features paintings, furniture, and decorative arts from the 17th and 18th centuries. Open May to October 31, Su-Fr 2-4. Adults 75¢; children 25¢.

Stonington is also home to Connecticut's first Federal-style lighthouse, an octagonal stone tower built in 1840. The *Harbor Lighthouse*, 7 Water Street, closed down as a working lighthouse in 1889 and today is a maritime museum. Open July to Labor Day, Tu-Su 11-4:30. Adults $1; children 50¢.

Founded in 1646 by John Wintrhop, Jr., the city of *New London* has gone through a series of dramatic ups and downs in its long history. It flourished as an international port until Benedict Arnold had most of it razed in 1781. But, by the mid-19th century, the city had made a comeback and was second only to New Bedford as a whaling port. Today, it is known primarily as the home of the U.S. Coast Guard Academy. There are, however, many historic landmarks and homes worth a visit. Begin with the *Downtown Historic District*, located between Captain's Walk, Bank, Tilley, and Washington Streets. The *New London Customhouse*, 150 Bank Street, was built in 1833 in Greek Revival style. Houses on nearby Starr Street date from this period and are in the same style, most without later alterations. On Captain's Walk, once the main street of the district, you'll find the *Nathan Hale Schoolhouse*. The Revolutionary hero taught here before marching off to war. The one-room landmark is open from Memorial Day to Labor Day Mo-Fr, 10-3. One of the oldest buildings in the district is the *New London County Courthouse,* 70 Hunting Street. This handsome Georgian building was constructed in 1784 and has served, among other things, as a hospital, a community center, and the site of the Peace Ball following the War of 1812.

Outside the downtown district, you'll want to see the unusual group of houses known as *Whale Oil Row,* 105-119 Huntington Street. These four homes, all Greek Revival from the 1830s and 1840s, have striking and similar facades, with two-story porticos and columns. Three of the houses now contain offices but the fourth is home to the *Tale of the Whale Museum,* featuring maritime exhibits and a fully rigged whaleboat once used on the *Charles W. Morgan.* Open year-round Tu-Su 1-5. Admission is 50¢ for adults; 25¢ for children.

The *Joshua Hempstead House,* 11 Hempstead Street, was built in 1678, which makes it one of Connecticut's oldest landmarks and one of the few old homes to survive Arnold's raid of 1781. The two and a half story house has been carefully restored by following the diaries of Joshua, Jr., who lived here until 1758. Many of the furnishings are original, including pewter, brass, chests, and cupboards. Open mid-May to October Tu-Su 1-5. Adults $1; children 25¢.

Still more artifacts are on display at the *Lyman-Allyn Museum*, 625 Williams Street, on the campus of Connecticut College. The museum features 19th century dolls, dollhouses and furniture, costumes, and silver. Nearby, at 613 Williams Street, is the *Deshon-Allyn House*, built in 1829, by a prosperous whaler. The house is a mixture of early Greek Revival and late Federal and features Federal furnishings. Both homes are open Tu-Sa 1-5, Su 2-5.

One final stop in New London. The famed *Monte Cristo Cottage*, 325 Pequot Avenue, was the summer home of literary giant Eugene O'Neill. The two-story frame house was the setting of two of his best plays *Ah, Wilderness* and *Long Day's Journey Into Night*. It can be viewed by appointment (203) 443-0051.

Just across the Thames River from New London is the city of *Groton*, best-known these days for being home to the huge U.S. Naval Submarine Base. You'll want to visit *Fort Griswold*, constructed between 1775 and 1778 to defend the shores of Groton and New London. It was here that Benedict Arnold successfully stormed the fort, killed the small band of men defending it, and then set fire to neighboring New London. On the grounds, there is a *Revolutionary War Museum* with exhibits that detail this bloody and important battle. Open Memorial Day to Columbus Day daily 9-5. The fort itself is open year-round from 8 until sunset. Free.

Where to Stay

The Inn at Mystic, Rtes. 1 & 27, Mystic, CT 06355. Tel: (203) 536-9604. Seventy rooms, with baths. Doubles run $40-$80 in winter; $70-$85 in summer for the Motor Inn. In the Inn and Gatehouse, doubles run $80-$110 in winter; $105-$135 in summer. From May to October, reservations should made three months in advance. Owners: Jody Dyer and Nancy Gray.

This is an Inn that has grown in stages and gotten better with each new addition. The Mystic Motor Inn and Flood Tide Restaurant were started on five acres of land overlooking Mystic Harbor and Fishers Island Sound back in 1963. In 1978, the Dyer family added antiques and canopied beds and increased the number of rooms. In 1980, they acquired an adjacent eight acre estate which gave them a handsome 1904

Colonial Revival mansion and beautifully landscaped gardens, walking trails, and an orchard to work with. Today, the Inn offers accomodations ranging from the modest to super deluxe. There are fireplaces, canopied beds, antiques, interesting bathrooms with whirlpool soaking tubs and spas. Wonderfully wide Victorian porches overlook the graceful gardens and Mystic Harbor. The Flood Tide Restaurant serves American cuisine with "a continental flair." Located one mile from Mystic Seaport Museum, the Inn has won four diamonds from the AAA.

Where to Shop

In Groton:

June's Antiques and Collectibles, 64 Hamilton Avenue, Groton, CT 06340. Tel: (203) 445-7523. Open mornings or by chance. June Franciosi. In business for over sixteen years, specializes in lamps, kerosene, and so forth, and also offers glassware, furniture, and a general line.

Toll Gate Barn Antiques, 381 Toll Gate Road, Groton, CT 06340. Tel: (203) 445-0533. Open daily 10-4. Ed and Bette McLaughlin. Primitives, Early American. Prices range from $1 to $500.

In Ledyard:

The Better Mousetrap, 279 Colonel Ledyard Highway, Ledyard, CT 06339. Tel: (203) 536-4759. Open by chance or by appointment. Cora Grunwald. This shop offers general antiques and collectibles from 1800-1940, with a concentration in pottery and baskets. Prices run from $10 to $5,000.

In Old Mystic:

Stone Cellar Antiques, 126 Route 27, Old Mystic, CT 06372. Tel: (203) 536-4344. Open every day by chance. Beverley Thayer. This twenty-year-old shop features Early American country furniture, housewares, and accessories. Prices range from $10 to $500.

In Stonington:

Trolley Barn Antiques, 145 Water Street, Stonington, CT 06378. Tel: (203) 535-1737. Open 10-5 Th-Mo. Raymond Izbicki. Trolley Barn sells silver, jewelry, folk art, ethnic artifacts, paintings, sculpture, and unusual one-of-a-kind small objects. Prices run from $10 to $10,000.

New Haven

Founded in 1638 by the Reverend John Davenport and Theophilus Eaton, a wealthy merchant, attracted by the town's location between Boston and "New Amsterdam" (New York), New Haven was at first an independent colony but in 1662 was brought into the Connecticut Colony fold. New Haven became a munufacturing center during the 19th century and it is said that Eli Whitney invented mass producton here. The most significant even in New Haven's history came in 1716 when the Collegiate School, founded in 1701 in Saybrook, moved here and occupied a building on the west side of the green. Today, Yale University is a major part of the city.

What to See

Yale University Art Gallery, 1111 Chapel Street. Founded in 1832 with the gift of some 100 paintings by the patriot artis John Trumbull, the museum is housed in two interconnected building--a 1928 Romanesque structure and a 1953 addition designed by early post-modernist Louis I. Kahn.

There are terrific collections ranging from ancient Greek and Egyptian artifacts to Impressionist paintings, from Renaissance master paintings to oriental ceramics and bronzes. A fine American collection, including furniture, ironware, pewter, and silver can also be seen. Open Tu-Sa 10-5, Su 10-2. Open Th evening 6-9 from mid-May to mid-September.

Yale Center for British Art, 1080 Chapel Street. Another Louis I. Kahn building houses the collection of British are-- 1,700 paintings, 7,000 drawings, 3,000 prints, and 16,000 rare books--given to Yale by Paul Mellon in 1966. Most of the work dates from 1700 to 1850, including great works by Stubbs, Turner, and Constable. Open Tu-Sa 10-5; Su 10-2.

Yale Collection of Musical Instruments, 15 Hillhouse Avenue. More than 800 musical instruments are on display representing the Western European tradition from the 16th to 19th centuries. Open September through May, Tu, Th 2-4, Su 2-5; June and July, Tu, We, Th 1-4.

Maine

Bangor

Ellsworth
Searsport
Belfast
Augusta   Blue Hill
Hallowell   Castine
Camden   Bar Harbor
Rockport   Northeast Harbor
Wiscasset   Deer Isle
Bath
Freeport
Portland
Kennebunk
Kennebunkport
York

Maine people, it is sometimes said, never throw away anything. It is an apt characterization. Whether it is a holdover from the Puritan attitude of equating waste with sin or simply Yankee ingenuity born out of the necessity of prodding a living out of an often harsh and reluctant land, Mainers are among the world's most resourceful people. The state provides a unique opportunity for visitors to see life being lived by people whose basic values and attitudes are not that distant from those of their rugged forebears two hundred years ago. From the town meeting and the red-cheeked lobsterman to the country store and the round-shoulder lumberman, Maine is living history and a delight for the student of America's past and collector.

Maine's physical beauty has long been a source of inspiration for artists and writers. Edna St. Vincent Millay first read her poems in public in Camden; Henry Wadsworth Longfellow grew up in Portland. Harriet Beecher Stowe wrote *Uncle Tom's Cabin* while living in Brunswick. Painters Winslow Homer and Andrew Wyeth both created some of their most famous works on Maine soil. One of the state's most recent appearances in literature is the bear named State-of-Maine in John Irving's *Hotel New Hampshire*.

For the collector, the "must" destinations in Maine are Hallowell, with its treasure-trove of antique stores; Bath, home of the fabulous Maine Maritime Museums; Portland, site of some of the most carefully preserved buildings in New England, and York's colonial village.

Augusta & Hallowell _____

Maine's capital city of Augusta is an attractive residential and industrial city of 21,164 souls and it does have a few noteworthy historical sites. For collectors, however, the real fascination here is the Augusta suburb of Hallowell, know widely as "the antique capital of Maine." Water Street, the town's main thoroughfare, may well be the only street in America composed almost entirely of antique shops. You'll come away with the impressions that nearly all of the town's 2,800 citizens are engaged in peddling the past. For antique lovers, this is one of New England's best discoveries.

What to See

Blaine House, 162 State Street, Augusta. The official governor's mansion since 1919, this two-story frame residence was built in 1863 as the residence of James G. Blaine, a Maine politician who served two terms as Secretary of State before being defeated in a presidential bid in 1884. Many of his family's original furnishings are on display, including a silver service recovered from the battleship nearly ten years after it was sunk. Guided tours weekdays, 2-4.

Fort Western, Bowman Street, Augusta. Constructed in 1754 along the banks of the Kennebec River as a defense against Indians, Fort Western is one of the rare examples of a pre-Revolutionary fort still standing. A log building that served as the commandant's home has been carefully restored and furnished with antiques; the two block houses and the stockade are reconstructions, completed in the 1920s. Guided tours are conducted from mid-May until Labor Day, Mo-Sa 9-4:30, Su 2-4. Admission is $1.

Hallowell Historic District. Most of the city of Hallowell is part of this treasure-laden district. Some 85 percent of the buildings here were constructed during the 18th and 19th centuries. Many of these early commercial buildings are now thoughtfully refurbished antique shops, chocked to the brim with virtually everything to tickle a collector's fancy. The dealers here are all friendly and helpful and if they don't have it, they know someone down the street who does. The most interesting sight in the district (if you can tear yourself away from the shops) is the *Hubbard Free Library*, founded in 1842, and housed in an 1894 Gothic building of native granite. Open daily except holidays, it houses the Hallowell Collection of early documents and photographs, and a 1602 Bible printed in Geneva. You'll also enjoy simply walking through the district and admiring the many lovingly maintained 18th century residences.

Where to Shop

In Augusta:

Campbell's Antiques, 405 Western Avenue, Augusta, ME 04330. Tel: (207) 622-5414. Open Daily, year round. Specializing in lamps, pine & oak furniture, Victorian glass, depression glass, baskets and primitives. Prices from $1.00 to $1000 to fit any pocketbook.

Margaret A. Buck, 5 North Belfast Avenue, Augusta, ME 04330. Tel: (207) 622-1839. Open 10-6 daily. Margaret A. Buck. Located near Blaine House and Fort Western, this shop features glass and china, linens, dolls and doll clothes, cellulose items, fans, and collectibles. Prices $1 to $400.

Pine Tree Stables Antiques and Collectibles, 1095 Riverside Drive, Augusta, ME 04330. Tel: (207) 622-4857. Open daily 9-5, except Su. Harold R. Bulger and T. Lois Bulger. A rather new shop, the Bulgers specialize in small items, glass, baskets, clocks, lamps, watches, and so on.

Red Sleigh Shoppe, 280 Riverside Drive, Augusta, ME 04330. Tel: (207) 622-1067. Open daily 9-5. Frederick L. Savage. Miscellaneous antiques and collectibles priced from $5 to $500.

White Barn Antiques, Riverside Drive, Rte. 201 North, Augusta, ME 04330. Tel: (207) 622-6096. Open daily 10-4. Eleanor N. Merrill. In business for more than fifteen years, this shop features Victorian accessories, paintings, small pieces of furniture, glass, and china. Prices are from $1 to $1,000.

In Hallowell:

The Antique Exchange, 130 Water Street, Hallowell, ME 04347. Tel: (207) 623-8188. Open daily 10-5. Betty Turney. Country decorative items, kitchenware, game boards, and advertising tins. Prices from $5 to $500.

Berdan's Antiques, 151 Water Street, Hallowell, ME 04347. Tel: (207) 622-0151. Open 10-5 daily, except Su and holidays. Charles M. Berdan III. One of the pioneers of the Water Street antiques revival, Charles Berdan features country antiques, pottery, quilts, weathervanes, and paintings. Prices range from $3 to $3,000.

D and R Antiques, 172 Water Street, Hallowell, ME 04347. Tel: (207) 623-2088. Open daily 11-5. Rowland J. Hastings, Jr. Clocks, china, glass, and furniture are specialties here at prices ranging from $10 to $1,000.

Hatties Antiques, 148 Water Street, Hallowell, ME 04347. Tel: (207) 622-0110. Open daily 9-5. Elery Beale. Another early arrival on Water Street, Elery Beale's taste runs to the Victorian--clocks, lamps, gold silver, coins, and jewelry. Prices are from $1 to $5,000.

Schneider's Antiques, 130 Water Street, Box 310, Hallowell, ME 04347. Tel: (207) 622-0002. Open by appointment only. Marianne Schneider. Another pioneer, Marianne Schneider specializes in antique toys and child-related antiques; mocha; butter and candle molds.

Two-And-One Shop, 190 Water Street, Hallowell, ME 04347. Tel: (207) 622-3800. Open Mo-Sa 9-5. Mahlong Thomas and Arthur Freeman. In business for more than fourteen years, Two-And-One features such exotica as beer cans and dishes, as well as furniture and bottles. Prices are $30 and up.

Bangor & Searsport

In its earlier, rowdier days, Maine's third largest city (pop. 33,000) was the largest lumber port in the world. Teams of lumberjacks felled giant trees in the forests to the north, drove them down the Penobscot River each spring, and spent most of their pay in a district aptly nicknamed Devil's Half-Acre. In the 1870s, Bangor mills were processing and shipping some 200 million board feet of lumber to the rest of the world. The legendary Paul Bunyan is alleged to have been born here in 1834 and you'll find a giant, strikingly ugly, statue of the folk hero on Main Street. The appeal for collectors and history buffs is the magnificent Greek Revival mansions--splendidly furnished--built by the lumber barons during Bangor's heyday.

Nine miles south is the historic seafaring town of Searsport, home to several fine antique shops.

What to See

Broadway Historic District. A treasure-trove of 19th century Greek Revival mansions built by lumber magnates, this district suggest that lumbermen knew how to live. Most of the grand residences are brick or frame, imitative of Brahmin Boston, and set well back from the graceful, tree-shaded streets. Notable among them is the *Isaac Farrar House*, built in 1843 in a cross between English Regency and Greek Revival styles, from plans drawn by famed architect Richard Upjohn. Farrar, a wealthy lumberman, had bricks shipped from England, roof slates from Wales, and mahogany from the Dominican Republic. Open year-round Mo-Fr 9-5 or by appointment. Admission is free. It's located at 166 Union Street. Just down the street, at 159 Union Street, is the *Bangor Historical Society*, housed in a two-story Greek Revival mansion built for a prominent business man named Thomas A. Hill. There are more than 20,000 items on display here, including portraits by Jeremiah Hardy, old lumbering tools, and a Penobscot Indian canoe used in timber drives. Open Tu-Fr 10-2 from April to December. Admission is $1 for adults, 50¢ for children.

Morse Covered Bridge, Coe Park. At 212 feet, this is the longest extant covered bridge in the state of Maine. Built in 1881 and nearly destroyed in 1961 before being saved by local history buffs, the Morse Bridge now spans the picturesque Kenduskeag Stream.

Penobscot Marine Museum, Church Street, Searsport. Four 19th century brick and frame landmark buildings house an extensive collection of ship models and memorabilia, antiques and furnishings, and ship models, illustrating the age of sail and trade. The *Fowler-True-Ross House*, built in 1820, contains wall hangings, paintings, and home furnishings brought back to Searsport by captains who plied the China seas. The *Nichols-Colcord-Duncan House*, circa 1880, houses the museum's library and two floors of fine paintings and furniture. The one-and-a-half story *Searsport Town Hall*, a brick Greek Revival structure, has shipbuilding tools, models, and a permanent exhibit on Down-Easters, large wooden boats built in Maine in the 19th century. The *Captain Merithew House*, circa 1816, a two-story Federal, contains an extensive collection of nautical instruments and pressed glass. Open daily May 30-October 15 9:30-5; Su 1-5. Admission is $2.

Where to Stay

The *Carriage House Inn*, Route One, Searsport, ME 04974. Tel: (207) 548-2289. Six guest bedrooms; three and one-half baths. Doubles run $32-42. Reservations are appreciated. AMEX, VISA and MC accepted. Owners: Nancy Nogueira and Susan and Bruce Atkinson.

Built in 1849 by Yankee Clipper Ship Captain John McGilvery, this nationally registered, Victorian house served as quarters for Army officers during World War II and later was owned by the late Waldo Peirce, the reknowned Maine painter, who used it as a summer home and studio. A frequent guest during the Peirce years was Ernest Hemingway, a wartime comrade. The house and grounds maintained as in bygone years are set on 11¼ acres well back from Route 1. The Carriage House itself contains collectibles, turquoise jewelry, antiques and memorabilia. No restaurant service is offered but seated continental breakfast is served in the fireplaced dining room by candlelight for guests. Nearby diversions include Acadia National Park, charter boat fishing, windjammer cruises, antiquing, golf and tennis.

Where to Shop

In Belfast:

Gold Coast Antiques, RFD 1, Box 142, Belfast, ME 04915. Tel: (207) 548-2939. Open daily 9-5 from April 15 to October 15. Vasco Baldacci. Located near the Penobscot Marine Museum, Gold Coast offers a general line of New England antiques ranging in price from $2 to $200.

In Searsport:

Better Days Antiques, Rte. 1, Searsport, ME 04974. Tel: (207) 548-2467. Open daily or by appointment. Bruce Frazee.

Specialist in antique furniture, walnut, oak, mahogany, and wicker.

Primrose Farm Antiques, Rte. 1, Searsport, ME 04974. Tel: (207) 548-6019. Open Mo-Sa 9-5 from April 1 to Novemeber 1; winter by appointment. Lix Dominic. Country furniture, primitives, quilts, early glass, china, and Shaker items.

Red Kettle Antiques, Rte. 1, Searsport, ME 04974. Tel: (207) 548-2978. Open daily 9-5. Dennis Middleswart. In business more than 16 years, Red Kettle features dolls, furniture, and primitives priced $3 and up.

Bar Harbor & Mt. Desert Island _____

At the turn of the century, Bar Harbor--located on the rocky northeast shore of Mt. Desert Island--was a favorite playground for seekers of rustic beauty with names like Rockefeller, Astor, and Vanderbilt. They came to this breathtaking place and built "cottages" of incredible opulence. Nearly one-third of the great estates were wiped out in a forest fire in October 1947 but enough remains of the past to make this an essential collector's destination. With its sheer cliffs and craggy coastline, dotted with white clapboard homes in villages like Northeast Harbor, Southwest Harbor, and Somesville, Mt. Desert Island is one of the most spectacular places on the East Coast, rivaling California's Big Sur for rugged charm. Nowadays the upper crust has given way to the L.L. Beaners on their way to Acadia National Forest, but Bar Harbor remains a symbol of elegance from a by-gone era.

What to See

West Street Historic District, Bar Harbor. One of the few areas spared the destruction of the major forest fire that destroyed hundreds of fine estates in 1947, West Street presents an easily-seen cluster of Maine's well-known shingle-style summer "cottages." The scenic beauty of this place was recorded in the 1840s by members of the Hudson River School, most notably Thomas Cole. Most of the cottages in this district remain private homes but a number of them--*Manor House, Thornhedge, Atlantic Oakes-by-the-Sea*--have become inns and welcome visitors. If you happen to be in town the third week of June, there's a great Antique Auto Show, featuring Stanley Steamers and all manner of Tin Lizzies.

Bar Harbor Historical Museum. Located in the basement of Jesup Memorial Library, this museum has an extensive photo collection recalling the town's grander days. Open in the afternoons daily between mid-June and mid-September.

Abbe Museum. Sieur de Monts Spring. When Champlain "discovered" and named Mt. Desert Island in 1604, the island had already been occupied for hundreds of years by Indians. Indeed, it is thought that canoe-borne natives from this island fought pitched battles with Vikings. The Abbe Museum records the lives of the first residents through exhibits, artifacts, dioramas, tools, birch bark canoes, and so on. Open daily May 30 to October 15 10-4 (except July and August when hours are 9-5). Admission is free but donations are accepted.

Where to Stay

Atlantic Oakes By-the-Sea, Eden Street, Bar Harbor, ME 04609. Tel: (207) 288-5218. 108 rooms, all with private baths. In-season rates (July through Labor Day) run from $71-$80 a day; winter rates as low as $28. Reservations for in-season at least one month in advance. Inkeepers: B.K. and J.P. Cough.

This elaborate old mansion, with its elegantly landscaped area overlooking the ocean, was built by Sir Harry Oakes, a prospector who hit it big with an Ontario gold mine. He moved to the Bahamas in the mid-1930s and in 1943 was found murdered in his Nassau home. His son-in-law was acquitted of the crime. The present layout of the hotel includes the mansion and adjacent motel units. The best rooms are a penthouse on the third floor of the mansion, which has two bedrooms, a living room, and a porch overlooking the ocean; and an apartment attached to the mansion which can accomodate a very large family. No restaurant.

Where to Shop

Pine Bough, Main Street, Northeast Harbor, ME 04662. Tel: (207) 276-5079 or 244-7060. Open by appointment. Jo

Anne Fuerst. Located near the Abbe Museum, the Pine Bough specializes in American pre-1850 antiques. Prices from $5 to $5,000.

Bath

One hundred years ago, this pleasant little town of 9,430 citizens was the fifth busiest port in the U.S. behind New York, Boston, Philadelphia, and Baltimore. A shipbuilding center since the 18th century, Bath's favorable location on a deep channel to the sea has been the key to its economic success. The town's 100 shipyards launched more wooden vessels between 1875 and 1900 than any other shipbuilding center in the nation. In 1890, half of the merchant vessels flying the U.S. flag were built in Bath. The city remains a shipbuilding center today; Bath Iron Works turns out modern frigates for the Navy at a twenty-four-hour-a-day clip. This is the best place in the state to get a real feel for Maine's seagoing heritage.

What to See

Maine Maritime Museum. The largest public museum in the state, its extensive nautical collection is housed mainly in three locations--with a delightful boat ride in between. You'll board the *Sasanoa*, a fifty-foot converted admiral's barge at *Percy & Small Shipyard*, 263 Washington Street, the only surviving wooden boat shipyard in America, now devoted to the restoration of traditional boats and the preservation of traditional boat-building techniques. Here, in the Apprenticeshop, you'll see young volunteers building and restoring old craft. The *Sequin*, the oldest registered steam tug, built in 1884, is also located here. From the shipyard, the *Sasonoa* takes you on a twenty-five minute cruise along the city's historic waterfront, past Bath Iron Works, to the *Sewall House*, 963 Washington Street, where the museum's most precious items are displayed. Intricate, highly polished ship models abound in this fine 1844 mansion donated by a prominent shipbuilding family. There are more than 15,000 fine and folk art items here and there's even a "Please touch" room where children are encouraged to clang a ship's bell and to turn a wheel. It's an easy walk to the "Winter Street Center," 880 Washington Street, which stages thematic exhibition featuring models, photos, and regional maritime history. Open daily 10-5 from May 14 to October 10. Admission, including the boat ride, is $5.50 for adults; $2.25 for children six to sixteen; free for children under six. A package price of $15.50 is offered for families with three or more children. The entry fee is good for two consecutive days. Highly recommended for anyone interest in boats, in Maine, or American history in general.

Bath Historic District. All of the museum's sites are located within this district and you'll want to spend some time roaming the quiet streets where many of the fine homes and buildings constructed during the 19th century boom period still stand. Notable among them: the *Captain William Drummond House*, next door to the Sewall House, which housed the town's first indoor toilet and the *Captain John Richardson House*, whose many residents since it was built in 1850 have produced only male offspring.

Where to Stay

Grane's Fairhaven Inn, North. Bath Road, Bath, ME 04530. Tel: (207) 443-4391. Nine guest rooms, one with private bath. Doubles run $30 to $40. Reservations should be made as far in advance as possible; one night's deposit required. If you stay a week, you get one night free. Owners: Jane Wyllie and Gretchen Williams.

Nestled into a hillside overlookng the Kennebec River, this delightful country home was built in 1790 by Pembleton Edgecomb for his new bride and was occupied by Edgecomb offspring for the next 125 years. A family named Gillies bought the house in 1926 and named it Fairhaven. They added more rooms on the west side in the 1940s but the east facade remains practically unchanged. Mr. and Mrs. George Miller acquired the home--and a twenty-seven acre plot surrounding it--in 1969 and spent the next nine years refurbishing the place. Current owners Jane Wyllie and Gretchen Williams bought the Miller home in 1978 and turned it into the country inn. No restaurant but $4 gets you a big country breakfast.

Where to Shop

The Recent Past, 17 and 32 Western Avenue, Bath, ME 04530. Tel: (207) 443-4407. Open by chance or appointment. Joyce Marco and Polly Thibodeau. Specialists in Victoriana, formal and country furniture, accessories, and textiles. Located near Maine Maritime Museum. Prices from $1 to $500.

Yankee Artisans, 178 Front Street, Bath, ME 04530. Tel: (207) 443-6215. Open Mo-Sa 9-5. An artists' cooperative, managed by Linda Szadis, this shop features traditional Maine crafts, including handmade quilts and wood carvings, and many others. Prices range from $1 to $400.

Blue Hill, Castine, & Deer Isle

The tranquil, breezy peninsula that stretches from Bucksport down to Stonington on Deer Isle is one of those special places in the universe that seems to have been passed over by modern civilization. There is Castine, with its stately white homes and tree-lined streets; Blue Hill, whose charm has attracted dozens of craftsmen and artists; and Stonington, the

quintessential Maine coastal village. There's great scenery and good shopping for collectors--particularly in Blue Hill.

What to See

Blue Hill Historic District. A village of 1,649 souls, Blue Hill sits atop a rise that looks out on the Atlantic and Mt. Desert Island. Most of the fine old homes here were built in the 19th century when Blue Hill was fishing and shipbuilding center. Today, the village is mainly a summer resort and its Main Street during the warm months one large open-air gallery. You'll find seascape painters, potters, and wood carvers galore. Don't miss *Holt House*, an 1815 Federal two-story frame dwelling on Water Street, now the home of the Blue Hill Historical Society. Its interior has been restored with period furnishings, artifacts, photographs, and other memorabilia relating to life in these parts. Open Tu-Fr 2-5 during July and August. Also not to be overlooked is the *Jonathan Fisher Memorial*, just on the outskirts of town. This 1814 homestead with an adjacent 18th century barn was once the home of Blue Hill's first Congregational minister. A genius of many talents, Fisher lived here for more than forty years. A number of his paintings and furnishings are a display. Open Tu and Fri 2-5, Sa 10-12 from July to Setpember.

Castine Historic District. This village of 1,287 residents offers glimpses of the days following the War of 1812 when it was one of the wealthiest small towns in all New England. Great homes are the attraction for collectors and history buffs here. You'll see fabulous Federals, lots of Greek Revival, and even some early Cape Cod-style houses. The *Wilson Museum* on Perkins Street has a good collection of prehistoric artifacts and maritime exhibits and also operates the *John Perkins House*, the only pre-revolutionary home still standing in Castine. Built in 1765, it is a fine example of Georgian architecture. Period furnishings add considerably to the house's charm, and there's a working blacksmith shop next door. The museum is open from late May to September 30, Tu-Su 2-5. The Perkins House is open in July and August We-Su 2-5. Both are free. Castine is the home of the Maine Maritime Academy and you can take a free tour of its training vessel, *State of Maine*, when it's in port.

Stonington. The principal town on Deer Isle, Stonington was once a great quarrying center and the pink granite used in many libraries and public buildings throughout New England was mined here. Today, the village is almost entirely given over to lobstering and fishing. Truly unspoiled, Stonington is the essence of the rugged character of early New England.

Where to Stay

The Pilgrim's Inn, Deer Isle, ME 04627. Tel: (207) 348-6615. Twelve rooms; three with private baths. Daily rate, with private bath is $65; semi-private bath, $55. Children are half price. Open from May 20 to October 23. Busiest months are July thru October. Owners: Jean and Dud Henrick.

Built by Ignatius Haskell, Esquire, in 1793, this great four-story colonial home is a Registered National Historic Landmark. Squire Haskell strategically placed his home between the Mill Pond and Northwest Harbor so every room in the Inn has a water view. Guest rooms are large and carefully preserved. Soft colonial colors and wide pine floors worn smooth by the passage of time conjur up the house's gracious past. Guests are welcomed by the golowing hearths from one of the many fireplaces throughout the rambling structure; the paneled parlor and dining room overlooking Northwest Harbor; the Common Room with its bay window and lovely view of the Mill Pond; the tap room painstakingly preserved to its wood paneling, and the barn that houses the summer dining room. All add up to an inn of uncommon charm. Rates include a hearty breakfast and a "creative" dinner, big on lobster, fresh fruits, and vegetables.

Where to Shop

Deer Isle folk are skilled in many handicrafts and the Haystack School in Sunshine is internationally known for its craft instruction. Good bargains in contemporary crafts.

Yellow Brick House Antiques, Water Street, Castine, ME 04421. Tel: (207) 326-8786. Open daily 10-6. Leila Badaro Day. Features American furniture, formal and country pieces, folk art, porcelain, paintings. Prices range from several dollars to several thousand dollars.

Camden & Rockport _____

Nestled at the foot of 1,300-foot Mount Battie with a vista out onto the island-dotted waters of Penobscot Bay, Camden is one of the loveliest villages on the entire New England coast. This was the hometown of Edna St. Vincent Millay and its natural beauty an obvious inspiration for many of her poems. In Camden's snug harbor are anchored tall two-masted windjammers, alongside sleek modern yachts. Seven miles south of Camden by Rte. 1 is the sleepy, picturesque seaside hamlet of Rockport. Both villages abound with shops and galleries, their windows decorated with flower-filled window boxes, and there are many delightful 18th and 19th century homes.

What to See

Old Conway House, Conway Road. A splendid example of 18th century rural construction, this rustic Cape Cod house is now home to the Camden-Rockport Historical Society. Hand-hewn hemlock beams, a double brick hearth, and wooden peg hinges ("trunnels") provide a testimony to the skill of colonial builders. Close by are an old barn and blacksmith shop. The barn contains a collection of early carriages, sleighs, unusual vehicles (a 19th century fire engine, and a locomotive once used to haul lime to kilns at Rockport) as well as colonial tools and farm implements. The blacksmith shop is fully equipped, including in "ox lifter" used to hoist the unwieldy beasts for shoeing. The Mary Meeker Cramer Museum--which is housed here--continas ship models and an extensive collection of period costumes. Open July and August, Mo-Fr 1-5. Admission is 50¢.

Camden Public Landing. A treat for fans of tall ships, Camden's great windjammers anchor here. Among them are the 137-foot *Roseway*, Maine's representative in the Bicentennial "Operation Sail" celebration, and "Adventure," star of the film "Captains Courageous." Nearby is a retired tugboat *John Wanamaker*, now a restaurant.

Rockport Marina. Summer home for Andre the Seal, a chubby little character who for the past twenty years has been doing his tricks for visitors at precisely 4 p.m. Andre spends his winters in Boston's New England Aquarium, but returns here during the warm months.

Where to Stay

Whitehall Inn, Camden, ME 04843. Tel: (207) 236-3391. Thirty-eight rooms, with private or shared baths. Open from May 27 to October 16. Until June 16, doubles run $42 to $52; after June 16, doubles with private bath run from $101 to $130. Reservations are accepted only for a specific number of days; there's a 10 percent discount offered by the month. From June 16 to October 16, prices include breakfast and dinner. Innkeepers: Jean and Ed Dewing.

This is the inn where young Edna St. Vincent Millay first recited her celebrated poem *Renascence* back in 1912. Built as a sea captain's house in 1834, the Inn has grown considerably since. Each of its rooms has its own unique charm. It may be a Currier & Ives print in one, a spool bed in another, or a view of the waterfront from still another. Antiques from several periods are spread tastefully throughout--a grandfather clock by Seth Thomas or Hoadley, a Queen Anne desk, an 18th century cabinet. The lobby and adjacent parlors are covered with a remarkable collection of antique oriental rugs, old pedal sewing machines accent the upstairs halls. Seashells, collectibles, and all sorts of treasures are utilized everywhere. Blessedly, there are no TV sets in the rooms but there are antique rockers on the porches that invite you to rest and enjoy the pure, fresh sea breeze that blows off Penobscot Bay. Particularly fine is the Inn's dining room where breakfast breads and muffins, pastries, cakes, and rolls are baked fresh every morning. Dinner specialities feature a variety of fresh seafood--baked stuffed shrimp, marvelous homemade chowders, broiled native scallops, fresh fish of the day. Formal traditions from the past are retained. Gentlemen are requested to wear jackets at dinner which is served by candlelight, classical music, fine linens, and great service. Expensive and worth it.

Where to Shop

In Camden:

Anderson Gallery, 10 Pleasant Street, Camden, ME 04843. Tel: (207) 236-2822. Summer hours, Tu-Sa 1-8, closed

Mo; winter, Th-Sa 10-4, Su 12-4. Formerly known as Ten Pleasant Street, this shop specializes in watercolor paintings ranging from $30 to $1,000.

Levett's Antiques, 69 Elm Street, Rte. 1, Camden, ME 04843. Tel: (207) 236-8356. Open daily 10-5. Georgia G. Levett. Features country items, baskets, hooked rugs, quilts, painted furniture, early glass, and ceramics. Prices from $10 to over $100.

The Richards Antiques, 93 Elm Street, Camden, ME 04843. Tel: (207) 236-2152. Open June to October 10-5. Sunday, Wednesday, and off-season by appointment. In business for more than thirty years, offering a fine general line and specializing in whale oil and kerosene lamps, and Woodstock lampshades.

Star Bird, 17 Main Street, Camden, ME 04843. Tel: (207) 236-8292. Open daily, 10-5. Ann Slocum. Decoys, baskets, tin, quilts, and pictures are the fare here. Prices from $5 to $500.

Town Shop Antiques, 28 Bay View Street, Camden, ME 04843. Tel: (207) 236-8230. Open summer months 9:30-5. Kitty Jenkins. Specialist in primitives, textiles, and china. Prices range from $5 to $2,000.

In Rockport:

Old Firehouse. Located near the Rockport Harbor, this old brick building serves as a gallery for the work of prominent Maine artists during the summer months. Open daily, June to Labor Day.

The Kennebunks

Located twenty-six miles south of Portland, the village of Kennbunk and its waterfront sister, Kennebunkport, offer a magnificently preserved glimpse of 19th century architecture, funishings, and lifestyles. Stately elms, emerald green lawns, and rambling white captains' mansions summon ghosts of the days when this was a prosperous shipping and shipbuilding center. Today, the villages are popular summer resorts and artists' colonies. There's good shopping in Kennebunkport's Dock Square, and both villages have fascinating historic districts.

What to See

Brick Store Museum, 117 Main Street, Kennebunk. Open year-round, Tu-Sa 10-4:30. Donation, $1. A modest two-story brick building constructed in 1825 that once served as William Lord's general store. Permanent exhibits include extensive seafaring displays, furniture, portraits, and carriages. The museum also operate the *Taylor-Barry House*, 24 Summer Street, and 1803 Federal-style mansion of interest for its period furnishings and stenciled hallway. Open June 15 to October 15, Tu-Th 1-4. Adults $1, children 50¢.

Dock Square, once the center of Kennebunkport's shipping activities and homeport to square-riggers galore, is now the commercial heart of the village. Highway 9 runs directly through this district which is home to dozens of small shops and restaurants housed in 19th century structures. The square is dominated by the *Soldiers and Sailors Monument*, built in 1909 largely through the efforts of Abbot Graves, an architect who lived here at the turn of this century.

Kennebunk Historic District is a predominantly residen-

tial area that runs along both sides of Rte. 9A from the Kennebunk River to US 1. The homes and churches in this area
reflect a wide range of architectural styles, including Greek
Revival, Queen Anne, and Federal. Most unusual, certainly, is
the *Wedding Cake House*, on Rte. 9A, a late-Federal-style residence completed in 1826, then completely covered with Gothic scrollwork in 1855. Legend has it that a sea captain who
lived in this house was suddenly called to sea just as he was
about to be married. The marriage was held but there wasn't
time to bake and decorate the traditional wedding cake. To
console his new bride, the captain promised to have the house
"frosted" like a wedding cake upon his return. The ginger-
bread lace that adorns the house and nearby barn was the
happy, if somewhat eccentric, result. The house is now a private residence and closed to the public but you can get a good
look at the exterior from the street. Also of interest in this area
is the *First Parish Church*, Main Street and Portland Road,
built in 1773, with an impressive tower added around 1838.
The square belfry contains a bell cast by Paul Revere and
Sons.

   Kennebunkport Historic District, an area bound by
Maine, South, North, and Locke Streets and the Kennebunkport River, contains architectural treasures dating from the
mid-18th century to the present. Notable among them is *South
Congregational Church*, built in 1824, from designs by Aaron
Willard of Boston. The church's massive bell tower is remark-
ably similar to that of the First Parish Church in Kennebunk.
Services are still held on the second floor but the ground floor
is a gallery featuring work of local artists. On North Street,
you'll find the *Kennebunkport Historical Society Museum*,
housed in the former Town House School. Exhibits are mainly
local history and genealogy. Next door in the *Clark Building* is
a splendid collection of marine artifacts and displays. Open
July-August, Tu-Th 1-4, Sa 10-12; June and September, Tu 1-
4, and by appointment. Admission is free. If you get hungry
while walking through the district, stop off at the *Olde Grist
Mill Restaurant* on Mill Street. Housed in an authentically
preserved corn mill built in 1749, the restaurant features such
traditional New England dishes as johnnycake, a corn bread
made of scalded meal, and baked Indian pudding. Open Tu-Su.

   Seashore Trolley Museum, Log Cabin Road, Kennebunkport. The most comprehensive collection of electric streetcars in the world, featuring more than 100 examples, including buses, locomotives, mail cars, and freight cars. A two-mile route provides a new experience for kids and a bit of nostalgia for older folks. Operated by the New England Electric Railway Historical Society, the museum is a must for collectors and trolley buffs. Open daily in the summer, 10-6. Admission is $3.25 for adults; $1.75 for children.

Where to Stay

The Captain Lord Mansion, PO Box 527, Kennebunkport, ME 04046. Tel: (207) 967-3141. Sixteen guest rooms, all with private bath. Doubles range from $79 to $99 a day, depending on season, and include breakfast. No pets, credit cards, or children under twelve. Owners: Bev Davis and Rick Litchfield.

Located in the heart of the Kennebunkport Historic District, the Captain Lord Mansion is one of the finest examples of Federal architecture in New England. Built for shipping magnate Nathaniel Lord in 1812, the mansion has a striking octagonal cupola and large rear ell, added in 1895. Although it was listed in The National Register of Historic Places in 1973, the mansion had fallen on hard times and was basically a boarding house for senior citizens when husband and wife Bev Davis and Rick Litchfield, two refugees from the world of corporate advertising, discovered it in 1978. With love and a lot of sweat, they have restored the mansion to its former glory, carefully preserving many of its original details and furnishings. In addition to the cupola, there is a four-story spiral staircase, a three-story suspended elliptical staircase, double Indian shutters, blown glass windows, trompe l'oeil hand painted doors, original "pumpkin pine" wide floor boards, a hidden gold vault, fourteen working fireplaces (including eleven in guest rooms), an eighteen foot bay window with curved sashes, and a hand pulled working elevator. Each guest room is lavishly appointed with period reproduction wall papers (one room still has the original wall paper), as well as period furniture. There are no phones or TV sets. The expansive front lawn is now called "The River Green"

and is owned by the Kennebunkport Conservation Society
which maintains it as an open area. Between May 1 and October 30, you'll need a reservation four to six months in advance.
For non-guests, Bev and and Rick give public tours beginning
at 3 p.m. sharp We-Sa. Adults $2.50; children $1.

Where to Shop

In Kennebunk:

J.J. Keating Inc., Rte. 1 North, Kennebunk, ME 04043.
Tel: (207) 985-2097. Open 9-5 Tu-Sa, Su 1-5 May to October;
November to April open by chance. This shop has been in
business more than thirty years and offers Early American and
Victorian furniture, glass, china, and reproductions.

Kennebunk Antiques, 105 Main Street, Kennebunk ME
04043. Tel: (207) 985-4808. Open Mo-Sa 10-5, March 1 to
December 31. Nancy Glendenning. 19th century furniture and
selected accessories, country and formal; especially china,
much Staffordshire. Prices range from $1 to $1,000.

Richard W. Oliver Auction and Art Gallery, Rte. 1, Pla-
za One, Kennebunk, ME 04043. Tel: (207) 985-3600, 985-
7040, 985-7466. Richard Oliver. Near the Brick Store Museum, this shop sells Oriental rugs, furniture, jewelry, glass,
silver, works of art. Prices range from $25 to $200,000.

In Kennbunkport:

Antiques at English Meadows Inn, Rte. 35, Kennebunkport, ME 04046. Tel: (207) 967-5766. Open daily, 10-5. Helen
Kelly. In business for more than thirty years, this shop features
primitive paintings, quilts, hooked rugs, and folk art. Prices
range from $30 to $600.

Cattails Antiques at the Ellenberger Gallery, Rte. 35,
Lower Village, Kennebunkport, ME 04046. Tel: (207) 967-
3824. Open all year-daily in the summer, 10-5; off season,
please call. Cathleen and Roger Ellenberger. Features country
furniture and accessories, folk art, paintings, wicker, baskets,
and marine antiques. Prices run from $5 to $1,000.

Gem Antiques - Geraldine G. Wolf, Ocean Avenue,
Kennebunkport, ME 04046. Tel: (207) 967-2089. Open daily
10-5, closed We. Gerri Wolf. This shop has been in business

for over fifteen years and specializes in antique jewelry. Prices range from $50 to $5,000.

The Goose Hangs High, Pearl Street, Kennebunkport, ME 04046. Tel: (207) 967-5717. Open 9-5 by chance, or appointment. Jean D. Pineo. Specializes in primitives, wood, tin china, glass, and "small things." Prices are from $1 to $350.

Old Fort Antiques, Old Fort Avenue, Kennebunkport, ME 04046. Tel: (207) 967-5353. Open 9-5 daily May through October; November through April by appointment. Sheila Aldrich. Country furniture, primitives, tins, advertising items, and English furniture. Prices range from $10 to $2,000.

Timberlee Antiques, 24 Peninsula Drive, Kennebunk, ME 04043. Tel: (207) 967-2647. By appointment. Bertha E. Timson. Specialist in figurals and Early American silverplate holloware. Prices from $15 to $150.

Windfall Antiques, Ocean Avenue, Kennebunkport, ME 04046. Tel: (207) 967-2089. Open daily, 10-5. Anne and Ken Kornetsky. In business over twenty-two years. Porcelain, American and continental silver, Orientalia, bronze, and 19th century art. No price range limit.

Portland

With a population of more than 60,000, Portland is Maine's largest and most cosmopolitan city. It is also its most historic town and residents have taken pride in preserving and restoring many architectural treasures from the city's 350 year history. There was a period, earlier in this century, when Portland seemed to be about to slip into the familiar pattern of urban blight followed by wholesale destruction of landmarks. A single event--the tearing down of a grand old Victorian rail station in 1960 and its replacement by a less-than-elegant shopping center--was enough to galvanize the community into action. Today, Portland is solidly on the comeback trail and one of the most interesting cities in all New England.

What to See

Congress Street. The best collection of historic sites and museums is located on this one long street which bisects the

downtown area. *The First Parish Church*, 425 Congress Street, was founded in 1674 and rebuilt twice on the same site during the 18th century. Maine's state constitution was drafted here a permanent exhibit traces Portland's history from the 17th century to the present. You'll find "Longfellow House," boyhood home of Henry Wadsworth Longfellow, at 487 Congress Street. The first brick house built in Portland (1786), the home today is a museum which contains furniture, art, records, and personal possessions of the Longfellow family. Operated by the Maine Historical Society, the house is open Mo-Fr 9:30-4:30 from June to September. The Society's own collection is housed in the Georgian Revival structure next door. It contains paintings, prints, photographs, furniture, pottery, and glass realting to Maine, as well as Portland. Open all year, Mo-Fr 9-5. Admission is free. the *Portland Observatory*, 138 Congress Street, was built in 1807 as a signal tower (as vessels were spotted entering the harbor, its house flag was raised to signal residents of its arrival). There's a great view of Portland and Casco Bay from the upper deck. Open Mo-Sa 10-6; Su 1-6.

Old Port Exchange. This waterfront district has undergone a dramatic change since the early 1970s when a few brave pioneers decided to open shops and restaurants in this area which was rapidly deteriorating. Inspired by their commercial success, other merchants quickly followed and today this area--which includes Exchange, Middle, and Fore streets--

is a delightful example of how an historic area can be saved by concerned citizens. There are beautifully preserved examples of Greed Revival, French, and Italianate architecture.

Spring Street Historic District. Portland's properous 19th century days as a maritime capital are reflected in the many splendid structures in this downtown district. Prominent among them is the McLellan-Sweat Mansion, 111 High Street, now home to the Portland Museum of Art. Maine's oldest public museum, this somewhat eccentric Federal-style mansion, built in 1800, houses the museum's collection of decorative arts and paintings, early glass, and furniture. The mansion costs $20,000 to build in 1800 and later sold for $4,500 when its owner's business failed during the period of the Embargo Act. Open Tu-Sa year-round 10-5; Su 2-5. Close by is the *Victoria Mansion*, a two-story brownstone built in 1859 by a New Orleans hotel owner. Now operated by the Victorian Society of Maine Women, the house contains splendid period furnishings (many of them original to the house), as well as marble fireplaces, French carpets, and lots of mahogany. The interior decoration was done by twelve Italian artists over a period of four years. Open Tu-Sa 10-4 from mid-June to Labor Day. Admission for adults is $1.50.

Stoudwater Historic District. Best bet in this district on the western bank of the Fore River is Tate House, 1270 Westbrook Street. Built in 1755, this gambrel-roofed structure was the home of George Tate, an agent for the King of England. Much of the original exterior material remains, and the interior contains period furnishings and artifacts. Of particular note is the fine woodwork, similar to that found in 18th century London townhouses. Guided tours Mo-Sa 11-5; Su 1:30-5 from July to mid-September. Tours cost $1.50.

L.L. Bean Store. No trip to Portland is complete without a sidetrip to Freeport, seventeen miles southeast. This is the factory store of the legendary sporting goods mails-order merchandiser. Founded by Leon Leonwood Bean in 1912, with $400 and an idea for a funny-looking rubber-bottomed hunting boot, the company had sales of $120 million in 1980 and its catalogue is seen by some thirteen million people in more than seventy countries each year. The store is open twenty-four-hours-a-day, seven days a week, year-round.

Where to Shop

F.O. Bailey Co., 141 Middle Street, Portland, ME 04101. Tel: (207) 774-1479. Open 9-5 Mo-Fr, Sa 10-4. Joy and Jack Piscopo. This 164-year-old shop offers antiques of all types and periods. Prices range from $5 to $25,000.

Venture Antiques, 101 Exchange Street, Portland, ME 04101. Tel: (207) 773-6064. Open daily 10-5. Isabel F. Thacher. General line, 19th, early 20th century antiques and decorative accessories. Prices $5 to $500.

Vose Smith Antiques, 646 Congress Street, Portland, ME 04101. Tel: (207) 773-6436. Open 9-5 Mo-Sa. Donald W. Harford. This shop sells copper, brass, cloisonne, champleve, and miscellaneous. Prices run from $10 to $4,000.

Wiscasset

One of Maine's most appealing seacoast villages, Wiscasset is a haven of Georgian mansions fronted by broad tree-lines streets, antique shops, and restaurants. Stroll through Waterfront Park and you'll see the abandoned schooners *Hesper* and *Luther Little* quietly deteriorating in the mud of the Sheepscot River where they've been beached since 1932. They serve as a reminder of days gone by when this was the busiest international port north of Boston. For collectors, this is a special town because of its many antique shops and a couple of the most unusual museums in all New England.

What to See

Musical Wonder House, 18 High Street. This stately 1852 Georgian dwelling is home to a marvelous collection of some four hundred 19th and 20th century mechanical musical instruments, phonographs, and music boxes, most of which are still in working order. Designed to reproduce music by means of metal discs or cylinders, these splendid examples of "musical automata" were highly prized by their owners as works of art. Many are enclosed in handsome handcrafted cabinets. There's a small shop where you can buy vintage sheet music, music boxes, and rolls. One hour guided tours are available daily from June 1 to Labor Day 10-5. Admission, which includes the guided tour, is $5.

Lincoln County Fire Museum. After you've seen the Lincoln County Museum and Jail, you'll be ready for something more cheerful. Ask to see the collection of antique fire-fighting equipment, including the town's 1803 hand pump. Open by appointment.

Maine Art Gallery. Housed in the 1807 Old Academy, this charming space now is used for summer exhibits of painting and sculpture by Maine artists. Open daily from June to mid-September; weekends, the rest of the year.

Where to Shop

Coach House Antiques, Pleasant Street, Wiscasset, ME 04578. Tel: (207) 882-7833. Open daily 9:30-5. William Glennon. In business for more than sixteen years, this shop features 18th and 19th century American furniture and accessories. Prices range from $50 to thousands.

Marine Antiques, Rte. 1, south of Wiscasset Village, Wiscasset, ME 04578. Tel: (207) 882-7208. Open Mo-Fr 9-5, or by appointment. John T. Newton. Specialist in marine art, carvings, scrimshaw, books, scientific instruments, military furniture, and related nautical items.

Serendipity Two, Middle Street, Wiscasset, ME 04578. Tel: (207) 882-6459. Open 12-4. William L. and Ethel Barnett. In business more than eighteen years, the Barnetts sell primitives, pine, pewter, sea chests, selected books, iron, and paintings. Prices $5 to $300.

Two at Wiscasset, Rte. 1, Wiscasset, ME 04578. Tel: (207) 882-5286. Open 11-5. Doris Stauble. One of the pioneer shops in Wiscasset, Two at Wiscasset has been selling Americana, folk art, and furniture for nearly thirty-five years. Prices range from $5 to $3,000.

York

Eight miles north of Portsmouth, New Hampshire is the historic town of York, first established as a Pilgrim trading post in 1624 and later named Gorgeana for English explorer Sir Ferdinando Gorges and chartered as America's first city in 1641. Ardent preservation efforts have made this one of the nation's most thoughtfully conserved communities. Virtually every street contains architectural treasures from the 18th century. Most of the worthwhile sites are within easy walking distance of the village green in York Village.

What to See

Emerson-Wilcox House, Lindsay Road and York Street. Completed in 1742, this large house has a varied history as a tailor shop, post office, and tavern. Today, it serves as a museum of local history and has a fine collection of decorative arts. Open Memorial Day to Labor Day, Mo-Sa, 9:30-5, Su 1:30-5. Admission $1.

John Hancock Warehouse, Lindsay Road and York River. The famous signer of the Declaration of Independence, Hancock was a wealthy New England merchant and on of his many properties was this shingled frame warehouse built in 1790. Operated by the Society for the Preservation of Historic Landmarks in York County, the warehouse today contains a good collection of old tools and antique ship models, among other Colonial-era artifacts. Open May 29-September 12, Mo-Sa, 10:30-5, Su 1:30-5. Free admission.

Jefferds Tavern, Lindsay Road. This saltbox tavern built in 1750 was once a stop on the York-Kennebunk stage route but today is home of one of the most interesting museums in York. Guided tours are conducted by hostesses in period costumes, complete with ruffled caps and full hoopskirts. Don't miss the upstairs parlor which is decorated with murals of York scenes, including the First Parish Church (second church in America, after Jamestown), Sewall's Bridge, and the Hancock Wharf. They were painted by local artist Adelle Ells in the early 19th century after the style of Rufus Porter. Open late May through September, Mo-Sa, 10-5, Su 1:30-5. Guided tours last thirty minutes and cost $1.

Old Gaol Museum, Lindsay Road and York Street. A brick and wood structure begun in 1653 and enlarged over the next two centuries as the demand arose. Now a museum, the old jail is believed to be the oldest English public building still standing in the United States. Rooms are furnished with period pieces, including a very fancy bedroom once used by a jail-keeper with obviously extravagant tastes. Its dungeons contain such lively conversation pieces as leg chains, manacles, and thumbscrews. Open mid-June through September, Mo-Sa 10:30-5, Su 1:30-5. Admission is $1.50.

Where to Stay

Dockside Guest Quarters, Harris Island Road, York, ME 03909. Tel: (207) 363-2868. Twenty rooms, all with private baths, in four buildings. Prices range from $32 to $76. Open from Memorial Day through Columbus Day. Reservations should be made as far in advance as possible. Owners: David and Harriette Lusty.

This charming inn includes the original homestead-style Maine House, dating from the 1880s, and three contemporary cottages, all with spectacular water views. David Lusty was running a marina here some thirty-five years ago and sometimes used the Maine House as lodging for fogbound yachts-men. Out of that grew the lodging business, which then led to a waterfront restaurant, serving luncheon, cocktails, and dinner. Thanks to the fact that his father was a prominent antiques dealer (he helped the Ford Foundation establish Deerfield Village), the inn has a number of excellent marine paintings, shadow boxes, boat models, and half models. Its fine collection of scrimshaw was given to the Old Gaol Museum of York Village four or five years ago. Breakfast buffet is served to guests only in the Maine House but the restaurant is open to the public. It specializes in New England fare, lots of seafood, roast duckling, and so on.

Where to Shop

George A. Marshall Store, Lindsay Road. Operated by the Society for the Preservation of Historic Landmarks in York County, this 19th century country store still functions as a shop, featuring crafts by local artisans as well as displays of historic merchandise and artifacts. Pewter, tin, and wooden dinnerware are among the traditional crafts for sale.

Gorgeana Antiques, Southside Road, RD 2, Box 292,

York, ME 03909. Tel: (207) 363-3842. Open all year by chance, or appointment. Norman C. and Julie Upham. The Uphams have been in business for more than twenty years and feature small antiques, mostly glass, china, collectibles and memorabilia.

Maritime Antiques, Rte. 1, York, ME 03909. Tel: (207) 363-4247. Open daily, 10-5. Chuck DeLuca. The specialty here is nautical, fire house, and military antiques. Prices range from $5 to $10,000.

Massachusetts

Greenfield
Deerfield
S. Deerfield
Pittsfield
Amherst
Hadley
Northampton
Stockbridge
Springfield
Brimfield
Sturbridge
Harvard
Lexington
Concord
Brookline
Waltham
Natick
Dedham
Worcester
Grafton
Newburyport
Ipswich
Rockport
Gloucester
Salem
Marblehead
Lynn
Cambridge
Boston
Provincetown
Duxbury
Plymouth
Sandwich
Dennis
Chatham
Hyannis
Seekonk
Fall River
Vineyard Haven
Oak Bluffs
Edgartown
Nantucket

Although other parts of the Eastern Seaboard were explored and settled earlier, it is generally agreed that America really began with the arrival of the Pilgrims at Plymouth in 1620. New England's earliest permanent settlements were established here. The Plymouth Colony was followed within ten years by the founding of a Puritan settlement at Boston; other communities were quickly formed at Salem, New Bedford, Sandwich, and other coastal locations. Fortunately for the collector and serious student of history, a remarkable number of 17th and 18th century dwellings still exist in these early townships.

Boston's reputation as an art center has been recognized since the 19th century when the city was nicknamed the "Athens of America" because of its extraordinary gathering of artists and intellectuals. In recent years, it has also become famous as a medical center. Institutions like the Massachusetts General Hospital and Peter Ben Brigham are internationally known centers of medical research and innovation.

No state in New England has more to see and do for the collector. You could literally spend a month exploring the historic sites and antique shops of Boston alone. Plymouth, Historic Deerfield, Stockbridge, Old Sturbridge Village, Cape Ann, Cape Cod, Hancock Shaker Village--the list goes on. Massachusetts has been blessed by a populace that appreciates the past and has gone to extraordinary lengths to preserve it.

Boston, the Puritan's "city on the hill" was meant to be a beacon to the world. It has succeeded in that role to a degree that the early settlers could scarcely have dreamed possible.

Boston & Environs _____

As the hub of a metropolitan area with a population today of over two million, Boston holds an unequaled place in the history of the United States. Seeking to carve a New Jerusalem out of the forbidding wilderness, the "city upon a hill" was founded in the 1630s and in the words of the Commonwealth's first governor John Winthrop, was to serve as a beacon of light to the rest of the western world, an example of God's true kingdom on earth. Throughout the 150 years of the Colonial period and, of course, during and after the Revolution itself, citizens of Boston and its outlying areas were in the forefront of the unfolding American saga. Even today, local municipalities spend more money on maintaining historic sites and buildings and commemorating their proud and independent heritage than any other region in the country.

What to See

Back Bay. Boston is best approached as a city of neighborhoods, each with its own distinctive local flavor, architectural styles, and points of interest. Located at Copley Square in the heart of this elegant district of stately brick mansions, outdoor cafes, art galleries, and antique shops is the *Boston Public Library*. Designed by architect Charles McKim at the end of the 19th century, the Renaissance Revival structure boasts rugged granite walls, arched windows, and detailed friezes. Open Mo-Fr 9-9, Sa 9-6. Free admission. Nearby is the *Massachusetts Historical Society*, the country's oldest such organization, located at 1154 Boylston Street. Its collection includes numerous rare objects and artifacts from the city's illustrious past. Open Mo-Fr 9-4:45. Admission is free.

Beacon Hill is one of Boston's most picturesque districts. The cobblestone streets, narrow lanes, and residential ambiance give the neighborhood an old-world charm. Like many of the surrounding dwellings, the *Nichols House Museum*, 55 Mount Vernon Street, is a Federal-style red brick townhouse. Designed by architect Charles Bulfinch in 1803, this home established the pattern for the neighborhood for the next several decades. The museum now houses antiques gathered from many areas of the globe. Open Mo, We, Sa 1-5. Admission is

$1. The Society for the Preservation of New England Antiquities is headquartered in another Bulfinch structure, the *First Harrison Gray Otis House*, 141 Cambridge Street. The interior has been restored with the kind of furnishings, fabrics, and decorative arts popular in the early 1800s. Open Mo-Fr 9-5, with guided tours at 10, 11, 1, 2 and 3. Admission charge is $2 for adults. The *Second Harrison Gray Otis House*, 85 Mount Vernon Street, is another Bulfinch residence designed for the distinguished Otis family in 1800, four years after the first. This magnificent Federal brick townhouse is three stories high; set back from the curb and apart from the houses next to it, it excludes an air of understated majesty. Impressive architectural details include a wooden balustrade, octagonal wood cupola, and graceful bay windows.

Quincy Market is currently Boston's leading tourist attraction. The three main buildings have been around since 1825, but for much of the present century they lay in disuse. Renovated less than ten years ago by The Rouse Company (which built Columbia, MD and also renovated the Baltimore waterfront), the historic site is now teeming with food shops, restaurants, and boutiques of all kinds, with a plethora of craftsmen and traders displaying their wares. John Adams dubbed nearby *Faneuil Hall* the "cradle of liberty" because of the volatile town meetings held here during the Revolutionary period. Commissioned and donated to the city by merchant Peter Faneuil in 1742, the building burned down twenty years later and was raised once more with meticulous attention to the original. The shining pearl of the redevelopment, the Hall is today the prime attraction in the Quincy Market area. The first floor has always been a market, and is open daily from 9-5. The meeting room on the second floor is open Mo-Fr 9-5, Sa 9-12, and Su 1-5. A military museum which occupies the third floor is open Mo-Fr 10-4. Admission to all three levels is free.

The Common & Environs. This central district contains more historic buildings than any other single area in the United States. On July 18, 1776, the people of Boston gathered under the balcony of the *Old State House*, 206 Washington Street, to hear the first public reading of the Declaration of Independence, an event reenacted every July 4th. This Georgian red brick landmark was built in 1713, making it one of the oldest public structures still standing in the country. The square in front was the site of the Boston Massacre in 1770, when British troops fired on a crowd of patriots, killing five. Threatened with demolition on several occasions, the Old State House has been under the protection of the Bostonian Society for the past one hundred years. It is now a museum with exhibits of local history. Open daily in the summer from 9:30-5; in winter Mo-Fr 10-4, Sa 9:30-5, Su 11-5. Admission is 75¢ for adults; 50¢ for senior citizens; 25¢ for children. Nearby, at the intersection of Washington and School Streets, stands the *Old Corner Bookstore*, constructed by druggist Thomas Crease around 1712. Over one hundred years later, the publishing firm of Ticknor and Fields took over the premises. During the mid-19th century, it became a popular meeting place for such leading literary lights as Emerson, Longfellow, Hawthorne, Harriet Beecher Stowe, and Oliver Wendell Holmes. The Boston *Globe* now maintains it as a museum, housing rare first editions as well as a desk that once belonged to Holmes. Open Mo-Fr 9-5. Admission is free. The *Old South Meeting House*, Washington and Milk Streets, built around 1729, first entered the history books on December 16, 1773, when citizens meeting inside, many of them dressed as Indians, stormed out of the church, boarded three merchant ships on the wharf and dumped their cargo of tea into the harbor. A two-story building with a wooden steeple atop a side tower, the Old South boasts a three-sided gallery surrounding a high-raised pulpit. Open daily April-October 10-6; November-March 10-4. Admission is 50¢. The *Boston Athenaeum*, 10½ Beacon Street, houses the country's largest public library. In addition to the collected papers of George Washington and John Adams, the Athenaeum is home to a vast array of Colonial documents, and rotates custody of Gilbert Stuart's world-famous paintings of George and Martha Washington with the National Portrait Gallery in Washington, D.C. Open June-September Mo-Fr 9-5:30; October-May Mo-Fr, Sa 9-4. No charge.

North End. This thriving Italian-American community was once home to some of Boston's leading citizens. The *Paul Revere House*, 19 North Square, was built in 1676 and is the only surviving residence from 17th century Boston. A two-story frame dwelling that is only one room in depth, it served as home to the entire Revere clan, including not only the patriot himself but his mother and twelve children from two marriages. The interior has been restored to match the style of the times. Open daily April 15-October 31 10-6; November 1-April 14 10-4. Adults 75¢; children 25¢.

Cambridge. Though less than ten minutes by subway from downtown Boston, the city of Cambridge--home of Harvard University since 1636--offers visitors an ambiance and historical tradition as rich, in its own unique way, as Boston itself. It addition to the Harvard campus, with its stunning blend of Federal, Romanesque, and late Gothic Revival-style buildings, Cambridge is home to several renowned museums with superb collections. Best of the lot is the neo-Georgian *Fogg Art Museum*, 32 Quincy Street, with indoor balconies overlooking the central interior courtyard that serves as the main exhibition hall. The two lower floors, surrounding the courtyard, are a replica of a 16th century canon's home in Italy. The Fogg's magnificent collections span all periods of Western and Eastern art, with notable examples from the Italian Renaissance, Impressionist paintings, and Oriental art. There is a particularly fine collection of Chinese jade and bronzes. Open Mo-Fr 9-5, Sa 10-5, Su 2-5. Closed Sa and Su in July and August. Just next door is Harvard's *Carpenter Center for the Visual Arts*, built in the 1960s and noteworthy for being the only American structure designed by the great French architect Le Corbusier. The *Busch-Reisinger Museum*, 29 Kirkland Street, is a superb baroque building with the finest collection of German art to be found outside Europe.

Works range from medieval to modern, with particular emphasis on 20th century masters like Max Beckmann, Paul Klee,
and Kandinsky. Open Mo-Fr 0-4:45, Sa 9-4:15. The *Francis
Russell Hart Nautical Museum*, 77 Massachusetts Avenue,
near the Massachusetts Institute of Technology, features an
extensive number of ship models and other maritime artifacts
of historical interest. Open daily 9-5. No charge.

    Concord. This Boston suburban city is known the world
over for two distinct reasons. On April 19, 1775, it became the
site of the first battle of the American Revolution, as British
soldiers and Massachusetts Minutemen confronted each other
on Concord's North Bridge. In the mid-1800s, the city became
inextricably linked in the public mind with the flourishing of
literature known as the American Renaissance. Since 1895,
the *Concord Antiquarian Society*, 200 Lexington Road, has
sought to preserve the town's heritage through its collection of
Colonial and early 19th century memorabilia. Among the
Society's prized possessions are those on display at the
Matthew Perkins House, including papers related to the lives
and works of famed Concordians Ralph Waldo Emerson and
Henry David Thoreau, as well as the lantern purportedly car-
ried by Paul Revere on his famous midnight ride. Open Mo-Sa
10-4:30, Su 2-4:30. Admission is $2 for adults; $1.50 for seniors;
$1 for children. The *Thoreau Lyceum*, 156 Belknap Street,
next to the Thoreau family homestead, houses displays on various facets of the famed Transcendentalist's life and career, as
well as those of his colleagues and literary companions. There
is a faithful reconstruction of his Walden Pond dwelling just
behind the Lyceum. Ralph Waldo Emerson's grandfather built
the *Old Manse* on Monument Street around 1765, and almost
a century later Nathaniel Hawthorne and his wife lived there
for the first three years of their marriage. The Georgian Colonial home derives its name from an early work titled "Mosses
From an Old Manse," that he wrote while in residence there.

    Lexington. Another of Boston's historic suburban
communities, this is a city rich in history. The Historical Society maintains *Buckman Tavern*, 1 Bedford Street, and has
restored the interior to recall its appearance during the Revolutionary period. A two-story structure, the venerable tavern
served for many ears after its construction in 1690 as a resting
place for travelers between Boston and outlying regions;

eighty-five years later, on the morning of the Battle of
Concord, it served as the gathering place for the Lexington
Minutemen. Open April 19-November 1 Mo-Sa 10-5, Su 1-5.
Admission is $1 adults; 25¢ children. Of even greater historical
interest is the *Hancock-Clarke House*, 35 Hancock Street. It
was here that Paul Revere found Samuel Adams and John
Hancock, who were visiting the Reverend Jonas Clarke, and
warned them of the British invasion. Hancock's grandfather, a
preacher and his namesake, built the original one-and-a-half
story rear ell as the parsonage of Lexington's First Church in
1698. Today, the dwelling is home to a fabulous collection of
antiques, most of them originally owned by the Hancock or
Clarke clans. Open April 19-November 1, Mo-Sa 10-5, Su 1-5.

   Salem. Located on the North Shore, the coastal region
stretching northeast from Boston toward Cape Ann, Salem is,
of course, well-remebered for its witchcraft trials and execu-
tions. The *Witch Museum*, 19½ Washington Square North,
presents thirteen scenes that trace the witchcraft hysteria that
gripped this community in 1692 and 1693. Open July and August 10-7; 10-5 the rest of the year. Admission is $2. *Witch
House*, 310½ Essex Street, was the home of Judge Corwin who
heard the pleas of more than two hundred unfortunate souls
who were brought here for preliminary hearings on witchcraft
charges. Open daily 10-6 from June to Labor Day; 10-5 March
to November. Admission is $1.50. On a happier note, the *Pea-
body Museum*, Essex Street Mall, is named in honor of philan-
thropist George Peabody, whose extraordinary generosity
helped the museum's orgainzers collect a rich and diverse
array of objects and artifacts that shed light on Salem's glori-
ous seafaring days and the natural history of the surrounding
regions. Open Mo-Sa 10-5, Su 1-5. Adults $1.50; children 75¢.
The House of Seven Gables is considered one of Nathaniel
Hawthorne's greatest works. The Salem residence at 54
Turner Street, thought to be the inspiration for the classic
novel, is one of a complex of eight dwellings maintained by the
House of Seven Gables Settlement Association. Initially built
in 1668 as a house with just four rooms and four gables, it
offers visitors an outstanding look at the construction materials and styles popular at the time. Open July-Labor Day daily
from 9:30-6:30. Admission, good for four houses in the eight-
house complex, is $3 for adults; $1 for children.

Marblehead. Another North Shore community, Marblehead today is a resort town and artists' colony. The *Colonel Jeremiah Lee Mansion*, 161 Washington Street, is a grand residence of prime architectural and historical interest. Commissioned by Colonel Lee, one of the wealthiest merchants in New England in the late 18th century, the Lee Mansion is unlike any other Georgian Colonial structure. It has a series of seven windows on each floor, rather than five, and is constructed of wood cut and molded to resemble stone. Since 1909 the house has served as headquarters of the Marblehead Historical Society, and has been restored with 18th century antiques and furnishings. Open May 15-October 14 9:30-4; other times by appointment. Adults $1.50; children 50¢.

Waltham. Located to the east of Boston, Waltham boasts two of the most impressive estates in the metropolitan region. *The Vale*, 185 Lyman Street, is a magnificent dwelling that can be reserved for weddings and other social events. Originally known as the *Theodore Lyman House*, the mansion is surrounded by lush and beautifully landscaped grounds. When the property was extensively renovated about one hundred years ago, only the ballroom and parlor escaped intact and retained the special atmosphere of the Federal style so popular in the 1790s when the house was first constructed. Only the greenhouse and property are open to the public. Open year-round Th-Su 10-4. Admission is $1.50 for adults; 75¢ for children. Waltham's other grand estate is *Gore Place*, 52 Gore Street, situated in the midst of 400 sprawling acres along the banks of the Charles River. Commissioned as a summer retreat by Christopher Gore, it was designed in 1805 by the French architect J.G. Legrand. With its central spiral staircase, Adams-style woodwork and—in contrast to the neoclassical standards of the day—rooms of diverse shapes and sizes, Gore House is an essential stop for those interested in early 19th century architecture and interior decorating styles. Open April 15-November 15 Tu-Sa 10-5, Su 2-5. Admission is $2 for adults; 50¢ for children.

Where to Stay

Hawthorne Inn, 462 Lexington Road, Concord, MA 01742. Tel: (617) 369-5610. Five rooms, three baths. Doubles run $80 a night. Reservation two months in advance in summer season; two weeks the rest of the year. Owners: Gregory Burch and Marilyn Mudry.

Situated on land that once belonged to Ralph Waldo Emerson, the Alcotts and Nathaniel Hawthorne, this Inn is about as historical as they come. Built in Colonial style in 1870, it is a stone's throw from all of the great sites of Concord. Rooms are appointed with antique furnishings, beautifully designed handmade quilts, wood floors graced with oriental and rag rugs. Original art works are displayed throughout, including antique Japanese yukiyo-e block prints, pre-Columbian ceramic sculptures, and prints and sculpture by the innkeepers. Little delights about: an 1810 Sheraton canopy bed here, an 1820 rope bed there, a 1790 envelope table, Windsor chairs, a Davenport desk, and so on. Home-baked continental breadfast is served to overnight guests. One of the best.

Where to Shop

In Boston:

Alberts-Langdon, Inc., 126 Charles Street, Boston, MA 02114. Tel: (617) 523-5954. Open daily 9:30-4:30. Laura Langdon, Russell Alberts. In business for over twenty years, this shop offers Oriental art, porcelain, furniture, paintings, and so on. Prices range from $100 to $10,000 and up.

Charles Street Trading Post, 99 Charles Street, Boston, MA 02114. Tel: (617) 367-9551. Open 10-6 Mo-Sa, 12-6 Su. Douglas F. Richardson. Features antique and used furniture, especially Victoriana, advertising, glassware, china. Prices run from $3 to $2,000.

Faith D. Rubin Antiques, 107 Pinckney Street, Beacon Hill, Boston, MA 02114. Tel: (617) 227-1158. Call for appointment. Faith D. Rubin. Specializes in English nautical, medical, scientific, and pewter.

Firestone and Parson, Ritz Carlton Hotel, Boston, MA 02117. Tel: (617) 266-1858. Open daily 9:30-5. Edwin I. Firestone, David Firestone. This thirty-seven-year-old shop sells antique English and American silver and antique jewelry. Prices range from $250 to $250,000.

Forever Flamingo, 285 Newbury Street, Boston, MA

02115. Tel: (617) 267-2547. Open 11-6 Tu-Sa. Forever Flamingo specializes in vintage clothing of the 30s, 40s and 50s; art deco, Fiestaware, 50s objects. Prices are in a medium range.

Howard Chadwick, Antiques, 40 River Street, Boston, MA 02108. Tel: (617) 227-9261, 437-1362. Open 12-4 most days except Su and Mo. Howard Chadwick. Offers 18th and 19th century antiques and decorative accessories. Prices from $1 to $1,000.

Louis D. Prince, 73 Chestnut Street, Boston, MA 02108. Tel: (617) 227-9192. Open daily 11-5. L.D. Prince. This antique shop has been in business for more than forty-five years.

Marika's Antiques, 130 Charles Street, Boston, MA 02114. Tel: (617) 523-4520. Open 10-5 Mo-Sa. Closed Sa during summer months. In business for over forty years, Marika's Antiques handles a general line of American, European and Oriental antiques including silver and jewelry.

Phoebe Antiques, 214 Newbury Street, Boston, MA 02166. Tel: (617) 262-4148. Open 9-4 Mo-Sa. Samuel Feinstein. American, English, French, Oriental furniture, porcelains, bronzes, and so on.

Samuel L. Lowe Jr. Antiques Inc., 80 Charles Street, Boston, MA 02114. Tel: (617) 742-0845. Open 10:30-5 Mo-Fr; 10:30-4 Sa (not open Sa in summer). Samuel L. Lowe, Jr. This twenty-year-old shop sells a general line of antiques specializing in marine antiques, paintings, prints, scrimshaw, and ship models.

Shell's of England, Ltd., 84 Chestnut Street, Boston, MA 02108. Tel: (617) 523-0373. Open daily 10:30-5. Eleanor C. Pumphret. This Beacon Hill shop specializes in English antique furniture and accessories. Prices run from $25 up.

Society of Arts and Crafts, 175 Newbury Street, Boston, MA 02116. Tel: (617) 266-1810. Open 10-5:30 Mo-Sa. In business since 1897, the Society offers contemporary North American crafts in all media with special emphasis on one-of-a-kind pieces of handmade furniture. Glass, ceramics, fiber, wood, and jewelry are included. Prices range from $10 to $5,000.

Vose Galleries of Boston, Inc., 238 Newbury Street, Boston, MA 02116. Tel: (617) 536-6176. Open 8-5:30 Mo-Fr; 9-4 Sa. Abbot Williams Vose, President. In business since 1841 (five generations in the Vose family). Specializes in paintings, 18th century through the first half of the 20th century, with emphasis on the American School with a few French and English. Prices start at $1,000.

Weiner's Antique Shop, 22 Beacon Street, Boston, MA 02108. Tel: (617) 227-2894. Open 10-4 weekdays. Paul A. Weiner. This eighty-six-year-old shop offers a general line of antiques. Prices range from inexpensive to expensive.

In Brookline:

Horse in the Attic Bookshop, 50-52 Boylston Street, Brookline Village, MA 02147. Tel: (617) 566-6070. Open Mo-Sa 10:30-5:30. Margo Lockwood. Horse in the Attic has a general stock of antiquarian books, used and rare. Prices from 50¢ to $350.

In Cambridge:

Bernheimer's Antique Arts, 52C Brattle Street, Cambridge, MA 02138. Tel: (617) 547-1177. Open 10-5:30 Mo-Sa. The Bernheimers have been in Harvard Square for over twenty years, featuring antiquities, Asiatic art, European art, primitive art, and antique jewelry.

The Games People Play, 1105 Massachusetts Avenue, Cambridge, MA 02138. Tel: (617) 492-0711. Open daily 10-6; 10-9 Th; 10-5 Sa. C. Monica. Specializes in games, including some antique games, toys. Prices run from $2 to $600.

Harvard Antiques, 1654 Massachusetts Avenue, Cambridge, MA 02138. Tel: (617) 354-5544. Open 12-5:30 Tu-Fr; Sa 10-5. Mrs. Fred Flett. Harvard Antiques, in business for more than twenty-six years, features Early American pine furniture and accessories. Prices range from $5 to $3,500.

The Music Emporium, Inc., 2018 Massachusetts Avenue, Cambridge, MA 02140. Tel: (617) 661-2099. Open 11-5:30 Mo-Sa; 11-8 Th. American antique fretted musical instruments: guitars, banjos, mandolins, fiddles, dulcimers, and so forth. Prices from $20 to $10,000.

Ten Arrow Gallery and Shop, 10 Arrow Street, Cambridge, MA 02138. Tel: (617) 876-1117. Open 10-6 Mo-Sa; 10-9 Th; 1-5 Su. Elizabeth Tinlot. Contemporary American crafts: blown glass, ceramics, furniture, turned wood, jewelry, iron. Prices range from $1 to $5,000.

In Dedham:

Lannan Nautiques, 800 High Street, Dedham, MA 02026. Tel: (617) 329-2650. Open by appointment. Joe and Larry Lanna. In business more than fifteen years. Specializes in ship models. Prices from $50 to $5,000.

In Lexington:

The Toadstool, 1632 Massachusetts Avenue, Lexington, MA 02173. Tel: (617) 861-6096. Open 9-5 Mo-Sa. Kim C. Fillmore. The Toadstool sells antique clothes, linens, quilts, new clothes, and new clothes and accessories made from old textiles. Prices run from $10 to $500.

In Lynn:

The Gumball Emporium, 57 Newhall Street, Lynn, MA 01902. Tel: (617) 599-5836. Open by appointment. Nancy Bergendahl. Gumball and other coin operated machines and related items. Prices start at $25.

In Marblehead:

Black Goose Antiques, 28 Atlantic Avenue, Marblehead, MA 01945. Tel: (617) 639-0465. Open Tu-Sa afternoons. Jean A. Lee. This shop features unusual furniture, glass, clocks, silver, lamps, handpainted pillows, cards, and so forth. Prices range from $5 to $600.

Brass Burnishing, 118 Pleasant Street, Marblehead, MA 01945. Tel: (617) 631-0648. Open daily 9-5. Jim Carey. Brass Burnishing sells antique brass, copper, and lighting fixtures; also, specializes in restoration and polishing of antique brass and copper items. Prices are variable.

Brass 'n Bounty, 68 Front Street, Marblehead, MA 01945. Tel: (617) 631-1703. Open 10-5 daily. Maryanne and Richard Dermody. Specializes in nautical instruments, old brass scales, birdcages, and lighting. Prices run from $5 to $2,000.

Cargo Unlimited, 82 Washington Street, Marblehead, MA 01945. Tel: (617) 631-1112. Open 10-5 Mo-Sa; 1-5 Su. Christina Ryke, Suzanne Farrell. Cargo Unlimited offers funiture, nautical, paintings, glass, china, brass, copper, and so on. Full price range.

The Good Buy - 5 Honest Ladies, 120 Pleasant Street, Marblehead, MA 01945. Tel: (617) 631-7555. Open 10-5:30

Mo-Sa, 1-5 Su. J. McComb, E. O'Dell, E. Wilson, B. Babine, R. Herman. Features all kinds of collectibles, oak, mahogany, and pine furniture, jewelry, Oriental rugs, china, glass. Prices from 50¢ to $5,000.

Sacks Antiques, 38 State Street, Marblehead, MA 01945. Tel: (617) 631-0770. Open daily 10:30-5. Stanley S. Sacks. In business for over seventy-one years, this shop specializes in furniture, china, silver. Prices start at $10.

In Natick:

Carriage House Antiques, 314 North Main Street, Rte. 27, Natick, MA 01760. Tel: (617) 653-6188. Open daily 11-5. Julie and Sharon Stevens. In business for more than twenty years. Country and formal furniture, primitives, oddities. Prices start at 50¢.

In Waltham:

Antiques 'n Oddities, 461A Main Street, Waltham, MA 02154. Tel: (617) 891-9456. Open 9-5 Mo-Sa. Irving and Edith Newman. This fifteen-year-old shop specializes in sterling flatware and silverplate matching, china, glass, furniture. Prices range from $10 to $500.

Holly Hill Antiques, 48 Weston Street, Rte. 20, Waltham, MA 02154. Tel: (617) 891-0300. Open daily 9-5. M. Beckwith. In business for over eighteen years. This shop offers a comprehensive line of antiques with a wide price range.

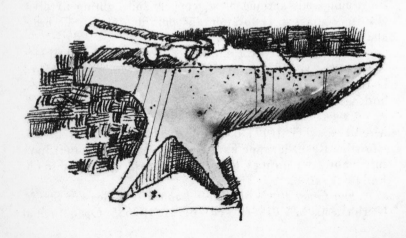

Cape Ann

Jutting into the Atlantic from the northeast edge of Mass-achusetts, Cape Ann is a region whose beauty and colorful history may be unequalled anywhere in the state. In all of the towns and cities along the shore, the sea has exerted a vital influence on the architecture, lifestyle, and economic pursuits of Cape Ann communities. And the stunning natural landscape makes it a popular vacation spot for those seeking to combine educational experiences with recreational pursuits.

What to See

Gloucester. In this small village at the easternmost tip of Cape Ann, you'll find *Beauport*, 70 Eastern Point Boulevard, a forty-room mansion that started out, in 1907, as just a modest summer cottage. The owner, Henry Davis Sleeper, was an inveterate collector of 18th and 19th century artifacts and antiques, and until his death in 1934 he continued to add on extra rooms to house his latest acquisitions. Built on a granite promontory with a spectacular view of the harbor, *Beauport* is open from May 15-September 18, Mo-Fr 10-4; September 19-October 31, Mo-Fr 10-4 and Sa-Su 1-4. Admission is $3 for adults; $1.50 for children. Another unqiue residence is *Hammond Castle*, 80 Hesperus Avenue. Built in 1926, it now serves as a museum and is ideal for those interested in antiquities from the Middle Ages and the Renaissance. The oringinal owner, John Jay Hammond, was an inventor and electronics entrepreneur, and the grandeur of the castle is testament to his genius. Two of its prime attractions are a coutyard patterned after medieval architectural styles and a massive organ with 8,600 pipes that is a full eight stories high. Open daily June 1-October 1, 1-5; October to May, We, Fr-Su 1-5, Th 1-5 and 6-9. Admission is $2 for adults; $1 for children unaccompanied by an adult. The *Captain Elias Davis House*, 27 Pleasant Street, dates from the 19th century and is now the home of the Cape Ann Historical Association. It houses a collection rich in artwork, china, silver, and textiles, along with documents for research purposes. Open daily June 1-October 1, 1-5; October-May, We, Fr-Su 1-5, Th 1-5 and 6-9. Admission is the same as for the Hammond Castle Museum.

Rockport. This community, reknowned for its talented artist colony, attracts a multitude of visitors every spring and summer weekend. Most of the visitors spend at least part of their stay along Bearskin Neck, a strip of commercial eating and drinking spots that was formerly the center of the community's flourishing fishing industry. *Motif No. 1*, a schooner destroyed by the Blizzard of '78, has been replaced by an exact reproduction of the vessel stationed on Bradley Wharf. The *Rockport Art Association*, 12 Main Street, is located in the *1787 Tavern*, at the heart of the city's *Downtown Main Street Historic District*. Bounded by Main, Cleaves, Jewett, and School Streets, this area was in its heyday from the 18th through the mid-19th centuries. In 1856, followers of Carrie Nation stormed the Tavern and other drinking establishments with axes to smash the beer kegs. They were arrested, tried, and to the delight of some and the outrage of others, were handily acquitted. On the south side of Main Street stands the *1803 Congregational Church*. The cannon on the lawn is the one used by British troops to bomb the structure during the War of 1812. The resulting damage—a hole in the bell tower. The *Sewall-Scripture House*, 40 King Street, today a museum, houses Indian artifacts, Colonial toys, and implements used to cut and transport granite from nearby quarries. Open daily July 1-Labor Day, 2-5. Free admission.

Where to Stay

Morrill Place, 209 High Street, Newburyport, MA 01950. Tel: (617) 462-2808. Ten rooms, five baths. Daily rates range from $31.50 to $48 and include continental breakfast. Reservations required as far in advance as possible. Owner: RoseAnn Hunter.

Although *Morrill Place* has been in business for just six years, the building itself is a twenty-six-room estate constructed in 1806. It features twelve working fireplaces, ninety-six windows and stairs with six-inch risers, designed in the days when women wore hooped skirts. Guests are served afternoon tea in a setting resplendent with antiques and period art objects. Very good experience for collectors.

Ralph Waldo Emerson, One Cathedral Avenue, Rockport, MA 01966. Tel: (617) 546-6321. Thirty-seven rooms, with baths. Daily rates run from $45-$75 European plan; $79-$ 109, modified American plan in season. Reservations needed as far in advance as possible. Owner: Frederick Wemyss. Manager: Gary Wemyss.

Surely the only hotel in America named Ralph, this mansion has been an inn since the mid-1800s and has flourished in the past nineteen years under its present ownership. Many of the rooms boast poster beds, while the lobby and dining rooms, with their beamed ceilings and Ionic capitaled pilasters are excellent examples of the Greek Revival style. Specialty of the Inn's restaurant is fresh lobster.

Where to Shop

In Gloucester:
Burke's Bazaar, 512 Essex Avenue, Gloucester, MA 01930. Tel: (617) 283-4538. Open daily 9-5. P. E. Pynn. In business for more than thirty-three years. Entire contents of homes. Prices range from 50¢ to $1,000.

In Ipswich:
Hilda Knowles Antiques, 207 High Street, Rte. 1A, Ipswich, MA 01938. Tel: (617) 356-4561. Open daily 11-5. Hilda Knowles. This fifteen-year-old shop sells a general line, "a little of everything," glass, china, dolls, and so on. Prices run from $1 to several hundred.

The Tuttles, 40 High Street, Ipswich, MA 01938. Tel: (617) 356-3780. Open by chance or by appointment. Patricia Tuttle. In business for over twenty-one years. Specializes in early tools of crafts and industries, Colonial accessories for Early American homes, folk art both old and contemporary. Prices range from $10 to $1,000 and up.

In Rockport:
Gallery One Seventeen, 117 Main Street, Rockport, MA 01966. Tel: (617) 546-2305. Open 10-4 daily May to October. Offers antiques, Oriental objects and carpets, European and American paintings. Growing collection of books. Prices run from $1 up.

Cape Cod _____

Cape Cod, that long peninsula that curves like a beckoning arm from the southeast corner of Massachusetts, is known today primarily as a summer resort region for the thousands of sun-seekers who flock to its communities and shores each summer. Like the rest of the state, however, it has a long and illustrious past. Indeed, in 1620 the first Pilgrims to set foot on the continent landed at Provincetown, though they quickly moved on to Plymouth. The Cape is an ideal vacation spot for travelers interested in visiting historic landmarks as well as the spectacular beaches and great seafood restaurants.

What to See

Chatham. In this quiet village on the southern half of the Cape, you'll find the Queen Anne "Stick Style" *Railroad Museum*, 153 Depot Road. Built in 1887, it is the peninsula's oldest surviving railroad station. In addition to exhibits on Chatham history, an old-time caboose adorns the grounds behind the station. Open from the last Monday in June through the first Friday after Labor Day, Mo-Fr 1:30-4:30. Admission is free. In the 1797 *Chatham Windmill*, in Chase Park on Shattuck Place, a miller reenacts the process of grinding grain which made the structure one of the central components of the town's economic life during the 1800s. Stage Harbor Road is the site of the *Atwood house*. This 1752 structure is now a museum which features displays of antiques, sea shells, and other natural and man-made objects indigenous to the region. Open mid-June to mid-September, Mo. We, Fr, 2-5. Admission $1 adults; 50¢ children, aged twelve and under.

Sandwich. Obviously the best place on Cape Cod to examine the glassmaking tradition of Sandwich glass. Any tour of the town must begin in the *Town Hall Square Historic District*, the center of Sandwich's economic and cultural life from its earliest settlement through the 19th century. The community's livelihood rested largely on the manufacturing of glass, and the wealth of many of its residents is evident from the impressive homes and public buildings erected in and near Town Hall. *Town Hall*, itself, an 1834 Greek Revival structure, and the First Church of Christ, built fifteen years later, are two superb examples. Also on the Square is the *Sandwich Glass Museum*, 129 Main Street, home of what is perhaps the country's most extensive collection of colored and lacy Sandwich glass. Open daily April 1-November 1, 9:30-4:30. Admission is $1.50 adults; 50¢ children.

The Historic District boasts several other sites of architectural and cultural interest. The interior of the *Old Hoxie House*, constructed in 1637, has been restored with furnishings from the 1600s. The Water Street residence is thought to be the Cape's oldest. Open June 18-September 30, Mo-Sa 10-5, Su 1-5. Further down the block is the *Thornton Burgess Museum*, dedicated to the memory and talent of this author of children's stories. On display with many literary papers are the Harrison Cady drawings that accompanied the original editions. The museum, along with the fifty-six-acre "Briarpatch Nature Trail" nearby, is open from June 17-mid-November, Mo-Sa 10-4, Su 1-4.

For doll house enthusiasts, the *Yesteryears Museum*, at Maine and River Streets, is a must stop with its handsome collection of antique dolls and miniatures.

Sandwich is also the home of the *Heritage Plantation of Sandwich*, founded in 1969 on Grove Street. The eclectic assortment of historical artifacts and exhibits spread out over seventy-six acres continues to grow. Current displays of note include a seventy-year-old carousel, a folk art collection, an operating windmill from 1800, antique automobiles and firearms, and miniature soldiers. Open daily May-October 10-5. Admission is $3 for adults; $1 children.

Provincetown. The Cape's most famous town is noted primarily for its sand dunes, artists' colony, and summer atmosphere. However, the *Provincetown Heritage Museum*, Commercial and Center Streets, established during the Bicentennial festivities in 1976, offers visitors a glimpse of the village's colorful past. Displays in the 1860 Methodist Church housing the museum include antique fire-fighting artifacts, an example of an early 20th century kitchen, and an exhibit celebrating the community's traditionally lucrative fishing industry. Open June 12-Columbus Day daily 10-6. Admission for adults is $1.

Where to Shop

In Chatham:

Yankee Ingenuity, 525 Main Street, Chatham, MA 02633. Tel: (617) 945-1288. Open 10-10 daily July and August; off season Mo-Sa 10-5. Jon and Lynne Vaughan. Features 19th and 20th century brass items, restored brass lamps and lighting fixtures, reproduction lighting fixtures, nautical antiques and reproductions, reproduction brass, cloisonne, paperweights, and photographs. Prices run from $3 to $900.

In Dennis:

Staffordshire, 1170 Main Street, Rte. 6A, Dennis, MA 02638. Tel: (617) 385-3690. Open 11-5 April to October; by appointment year-round. Sylvia H. Hosley. In business for more than fifteen years, this shop specializes in 18th and 19th century Staffordshire figurines. Prices range from $50 to $1,500.

In Hyannis:

Carrousel Antiques, 25 Sherman Square, Hyannis, MA 02601. Tel: (617) 771-4060. Open 10-5 daily. Felippa Garrity. Near the Kennedy Compound. Offers antiques, decorative furnishings, art, and gifts. Prices are from $5 to $50 and up.

Stone's Antique Shop, 659 Main Street, Hyannis, MA 02601. Tel: (617) 775-3913. Open daily 9-6. E. Stone. This sixty-three-year-old shop features furniture, glass, china, brass, pewter, and silver. Prices from $5 to $3,000.

In Provincetown:

Doe's Treasures Jewelers, 174 Commercial Street, Provincetown, MA 02657. Tel: (617) 487-2190. Open 10 in the morning till 11 in the evening, May to October. Doris Kirshenbaum. Antique jewelry, watches, beads, silver, paperweights. Watch and clock repair. Prices run from $5 to $15,000.

Remembrances of Things Past, 376 Commercial Street, Box 994, Provincetown, MA 02657. Tel: (617) 487-9443. Open 11-11 during the season; off-season open weekends 12-5. Helene Lyons. Neon, etched glass, art deco, old advertising, jewelry, crate labels, posters, books. Prices range from $1 to $500.

In Sandwich:

Dillingham House Antiques, 71 Main Street, Sandwich, MA 02563. Tel: (617) 888-0999. Open by appointment. Jesse C. Leatherwood. In business for over sixteen years, this shop specializes in Americana. Prices from $50 to $20,000.

Fall River & Seekonk

Though Fall River suffered from a severe economic slump during the middle of the current century, it was a vital center of the New England cotton industry during the late 1800s and early 1900s. Masses of European immigrants arrived during that period to work in the area's cotton mills and Fall River and neighboring Seekonk soon laid claim to one of New England's most diverse populations. Today the area is regaining its status as a prosperous and thriving economic community and has also begun to rediscover its historic past.

What to See

Battleship Cove, State Pier. One of the city's prime tourist attractions, this pier is home to four American World War II combat vessels--the battleship USS Massachusetts, the submarine USS Lionfish, the destroyer USS Joseph P. Kennedy, JR., and PT Boat 796. You can tour the boats, attend films and lectures, and examine exhibits of maritime artifacts. Open daily 9-5. Admission is $3.50 for adults; $1.75 for children. Combination tickets for both Battleship Cove and Marine Museum (see below) are $4 for adults; $2 for children.

Marine Museum, 70 Water Street. The museum is a testament to Fall River's importance as a chain in the transportation network linking New York City and Boston. Travelers arriving from Boston by the trail service established in the early 1800s could catch the Fall River Line of spectacular side-wheeler steamships destined for New York. The museum houses paintings, models, and prints celebrating the steamship line. Open daily June 29-Labor Day 9-8; other times Mo-Fr 9-5, Sa-Su 10-5. Admission is $1.25 adults; 75¢ children. For combination tickets, see above.

Where to Shop

Leonard's Antiques, Inc., 600 Taunton Avenue, Seekonk, MA 02771. Tel: (617) 336-8585. Open 8-5 Mo-Sa, Su 1-5. Robert L. Jenkins. In business for fifty years, Leonard's offers American antique furniture, specializing in antique beds. Prices range from $400 to $4,000.

Martha's Vineyard

Martha's Vineyard is a short ferry ride from Falmouth at the base of Cape Cod. The island, the remnant of a glacier that covered the region 60,000 years ago, is steeped in history. The community was one of the great centers of the 19th century whaling industry. Today, tourism is the island's leading business. Indeed, many of the current real estate dealers, restauranteurs, and hotel owners are descendants of natives active in the thriving maritime ventures of the past. Martha's Vineyard is also the home of a growing number of well-known writers, artists, musicians, and actors.

What to See

Edgartown. The most popular and picturesque of the island villages, its sea-faring past is the focus of exhibits at the

Dukes County Historical Society. The Society is located at Cooke and School Streets in the *Thomas Cooke House*, a dwelling constructed by shipbuilders in 1765, which explains its wide floors and slanted beams. In addition to scrimshaw, model ships, and whaling equipment, the Society's collection also includes household artifacts, children's toys, glassware, and china. The *Cooke House* is actually just one of several facilities on the site; a research library stores documents and papers such as journals and ship logs; boats and carriages are on display in a shed, and a reconstructed lighthouse also graces the property. Open June 15-September 15, Tu-Sa 10-4:30. Admission is $1.

The *Old Whaling Church*, Main and Church Streets, today retains a small but loyal congregation. In its heyday during the mid-1800s, Sunday sermons here regularly drew a crowd of over eight hundred (rounded) people. Built in 1843 in Greek Revival style, the Methodist sanctuary has 160 box pews, a working organ over one hundred years old, and imposing Gothic columns. Located jsut next door is the *Dr. Daniel Fisher House*. The residence was constructed in 1840 under Fisher's watchful eye. The doctor was, in fact, one of the Vineyard's richest men. He earned his fortune from the sale of whale oil to lighthouses along the coast. The house today is used for office space, and is open during the summer of Mo-Fr 11-1 and 2-4. Admission, which also allows you access to the church, is $1.

Every Memorial Day, the *Town Dock* is the scene of festivities commemorating those who have died at sea--many of them, no doubt, crewmen on the whaling ships and schooners that used to dock here. The ferry ride to Chappaquiddick is only 25¢ per person.

Oak Bluff and Vineyard Haven. The island's two other main towns both have much to offer in the way of architectural and historical delight. The *Flying Horses Carousel*, 33 Oak Bluffs Avenue, is reportedly the country's oldest working merry-go-round. The carousel was originally designed for Coney Island in New York and was moved here in 1884. On nearby Circuit Avenue, Oak Bluffs' main walkway, are a host of antique shops, galleries, and boutiques.

During the summer, from We-Su between 10 and 3:30, visitors to Vineyard Haven can stop by *Seaman's Bethel* alongside the village ferry dock. On display here are memorabilia celebrating the island's early days when steam and sailing ships loomed on the horizon. Admission is 50¢.

Where to Stay

The Charlotte Inn, South Summer Street, Edgartown, MA 02539. Tel: (617) 627-4751. Twenty-five rooms, twenty-four baths. Reservations should be made as far in advance as possible. Daily rates, including breakfast, range from $75 to $175 in-season and $32 to $125 off-season. Owner: Gery Conover.

The Inn, originally the residence of a Martha's Vineyard sea captain, is a three-story white clapboard structure with a widow's walk on top. Many of the rooms include working fireplaces and are furnished with four-poster beds, antique chairs and sofas, and Oriental rugs. The paintings and engravings that line the walls enhance the Inn's picturesque charm, reminiscent of the 19th century during the island's seafaring heyday. So do the renovated whaling home next door and the carriage house out back, which has expanded the capacity of the Inn. French cuisine is served at the superb Chez Pierre; located on the first floor, it is open from mid-March through New Year's Day. The Inn also houses both a gallery and an antique shop, as well as being within easy access to the delights of Edgartown itself. As one travel writer put it: the Inn is no less than "a museum of art that takes boarders."

Where to Shop

Ayn's Shuttle Shop, Lake Avenue, Oak Bluffs, Martha's Vineyard Island, MA 02557. Tel: (617) 693-0134. Open 9-9 daily, May thru Oct. Also by appointment. Ayn Chase. In business for over twenty-eight years, Ayn sells all handcrafted, lace-woven items, pottery, paintings, woven goods, lampshades, leather, and woodenware. Prices range from $2.50 to $300 and up.

The Secret Garden, Circuit Avenue, Oak Bluffs, Martha's Vineyard Island, MA 02557. Tel: (617) 693-4759. Open 9:30-9:30 summer, 10-5:30 off season. The Secret Garden features wicker furniture, porcelain dolls, Oriental porcelains, pillows, silk flowers, jewelry from China and other parts of the world, Oriental paper goods and lanterns. Prices run from $5 to $500.

Nantucket

The glory of Nantucket's whaling days surpasses even that of Martha's Vineyard, particularly after the wealth of Japanese whaling grounds was discovered in the early 1800s. Captains and merchants built spectacular mansions, packed to the rafters with treasures from the Orient. In 1846, however, a fire devastated much of the town, and three years later many of the residents, tired of the long and arduous whaling voyages, headed west to pan for gold in the California hills. Only in recent years has Nantucket's historic value been redis-covered. The entire town has been added to the list of National Historic Landmarks.

What to See

The Nathanial Macy House, 12 Liberty Street, is a 1723 clapboard structure with an added lean-to, similar to many of the Quaker homes dating from the early 18th century. Macy's father, incidentally, was the first white settler on the island. Open daily June-September 10-5. Admission is $1.

The William Hawden House, 96 Pleasant Street, is a brick residence with clapboard covering and is noted not only for its fine furnishings and detailed interior woodwork but also for being the island's best example of Greek Revival architec-ture. Open during the summer months daily 10-5. Admission is $1.

The Peter Foulger Museum and the *Whaling Museum* stand side-by-side at 22 Broad Street. The former contains exhibits on Nantucket's maritime history and its lucrative Chi-na trade, along with examples of antique implements, silver, and clocks. On view next door are artifacts crucial to the whaling industry, as well as a fully-rigged whale boat and forty-four-foot whale skeleton. Admission to first is $1; to the second $1.25.

The Friends Meeting House on Fair Street is the sole remnant of another of the town's early traditions. Before the influx of wealth and worldly sophistication that stemmed from the whaling industry and weakened its fundamentalist appeal, Quakerism was the religion of choice for most of Nantucket's residents. Today, the barren, stark structure is a museum exploring the Quaker heritage. Open 10-5 daily during the summer. Admission is $1.

The Nantucket Atheneum, Main Street, is one of the nations' oldest libraries. Though the original building was destroyed by fire in 1846, this Greek Revival structure was built soon thereafter. Open afternoons Mo-Sa.

Many of the island's historic sites are under the auspices of the *Nantucket Historical Association*. During the summer months, a $4 pass will gain you access to many of the sites of interest. For information on special events, operating hours at other times of the year, and additional island activities, contact the Nantucket Historical Association, Box 1016, Union Street, Nantucket, MA 02554, or call (617) 228-1894.

Where to Shop

Upstairs-Downstairs, 51 Main Street, Nantucket, MA 02554. Tel: (617) 228-4250. Open daily 10-5. Maureen E. Tellex. Specializes in Irish imports: clothing, china, crystal. Prices range from $2.50 to $1,000.

Val Maitino Antiques, 31 North Liberty Street, Nantucket, MA 02554. Tel: (617) 228-2747. Open 9-1 and 2-5:30 Mo-Sa; evenings and Su by appointment. M.J. Maitino. This thirty-three-year-old shop offers furniture, lighting fixtures, marine items, hooked rugs, weathervanes, eagles, decorative accessories, and so forth. Varied price range.

Pittsfield, Stockbridge, & Hancock Shaker Village

The Berkshire Mountains of Western Massachusetts, a hilly region boasting graceful and elegant patrician homes, has traditionally attracted numerous artists, writers, musicians, and those in other creative endeavors. Pittsfield is the area's

primary industrial center; however, the community and its outlying districts still preserve a heartfelt appreciation of the past.

What to See

Park Square Historic District. This area, which lies at the meeting points of North, South, East, and West Streets, retains much of its 18th and 19th century atmosphere and is a prime example of Pittsfield's determination to retain a connection with its historic traditions. The Federal-style two-story *Old Town Hall*, 43 East Street, where soldiers were recruited during the Civil War, was built in 1832; today it is the town's oldest standing public building. The Romanesque *Berkshire County Court House*, designed by Louis Weisbein and built in 1872, is constructed out of marble from nearby quarries. A third important structure with the district is the Venetian Gothic building adorned by colorful local granite and bluestone that in 1876 became the home of the *Berkshire Athenaeum*. Started as a public library, the Athenaeum today offers visitors a look at extensive literary memorabilia, including an impressive array of materials on local resident Herman Melville. Open winter months Mo. We. Fr-Sa 10-5; Tu, Th 10-9. Summer months We, Fr 10-5; Tu, Th 10-9; Sa 10-1.

Other displays on the town's past are on view at the *Berkshire Museum*, 39 South Street. Open September-June Tu-Sa 10-5, Su 1-5; July-August Mo 10-5. Admission is free.

Hancock Shaker Village, five miles south of Pittsfield on US 20 (also known as the Pittsfield-Albany Road). This restored village thrived from 1790, went into decline in this century, and was officially closed down as a Shaker community in 1960. Twenty buildings remain standing on the 1,000 acres left of the original 3,000. These include the twelve-sided *Round Barn* with an octagonal cupola and air shaft; the 1830 brick *Main Dwelling House*, with living quarters for over one hundred of the sect's members and a communal kitchen and dining room; the *Meeting House* with gambrel roof and segregated entryways for male and female inhabitants; and the *Sisters' Dairy and Weaving Shop* where the women produced domestic necessities, crafts to sell, and herbal medicines. Shaker Village is open from June to October daily from 9:30-5. Admission is $4.50 for adults; $1 for children. Special crafts workshops, lectures, and other activities are regularly scheduled. For information, call (413) 443-0188.

Stockbridge. The essential stop for collectors in this nearby Berkshire community is *The Norman Rockwell Museum at the Old Corner House* on Main Street. This beautiful late 18th century Georgian structure houses the only signficant collection of Norman Rockwell paintings in existence. The collection falls into two parts: Rockwell's personal collection and a group of paintings acquired by the museum during the last few years. Some the early drawings and paintings done for *St. Nicholas* and other magazines, as well as *Saturday Evening Post* covers and story illustrations are always on display. The *Four Freedoms* paintings and *Stockbridge in Winter* are on permanent display. A museum shop is touched with a supply of prints, books, calendars, and other collectibles that tastefully reproduce Rockwell's work. Also available are limited edition lithographs and colletypes signed by the artist. The museum is open daily 10-5, except for Tu, Thanksgiving, Christmas, New Year's Day, and a two week period at the end of January. Guided tours are conducted by trained docents. Admission is $3 adults; $1 children.

Another fine stop in Stockbridge is *Naumkeag*, on Prospect Hill Road, which was the summer retreat of the illustrious Choate family until 1959. The original owner of the 1866

Shingle-style mansion was U.S. Ambassador to Britain Joseph Hodge Choate. It was he who insisted upon the estate's meticulously kept and landscaped grounds. Indeed, visitors today are always enchanted by the Chinese garden and pagoda. From May 23-June 21, open Sa 10-5, Su 11-4; from June 28-September 1, Tu-Sa 10-5, Su and holdiays 11-4; September 2-October 13, Su and holidays 11-4. Admission to the house and garden is $2.50 for adults; 75¢ for children. To make reservations write *Naumkeag*, PO Box 115, Stockbridge, MA 01262 or call (415) 298-3239.

The importance of the Choate family in Stockbridge life is reflected in their sponsorship of the restoration of *Mission House* on Main Street. Built in 1739 as a frontier vanguard, it served as a classroom where the Reverend John Sergeant could pursue his missionary work among the local Indians. Later on, the dwelling served as an occasional retreat for the Reverend Johnathan Edwards, a brilliant and fiery preacher and on of the foremost theologians of the Colonial period. Open Memorial Day-Columbus Day, Tu-Sa 10-5, Su and holidays 11-4. Admission is $1.50 adults; 50¢ for children and students.

Merwin House, 39 Main Street, has been dubbed "Tranquility" because of the peaceful and calming influence of its Federal brick style. The Society for the Preservation of New England Antiquities maintains the house as a museum for visitors interested in superior period antiques. Open June 1-October 14, Tu, Th, Sa-Su 12-5. Admission is $1.50.

One of Stockbridge's most important artistic sites is *Chesterwood*, located on Rte. 183. The estate, dating from the turn of the 20th century, was the home of sculptor Daniel Chester French, whose famous statue of Lincoln stands in the capital's Lincoln Memorial. Chesterwood visitors can explore the Georgian dwelling, a barn gallery, the sculptor's studio, and an outstanding exhibit of French's sculpture displayed in the surrounding gardens. Open May-October 31 daily 10-5. Admission is $2.50 adults; $2 senior citizens; $1 children and students.

Where to Stay

The Red Lion Inn, Main Street, Stockbridge, MA 01262. Tel: (413) 298-5545. One hundred rooms; seventy-two with private bath. Daily rates range from $35 to $120. Depending upon the season, reservations should be made well in advance. Owners: John and Jane Fitzpatrick.

The Red Lion has been welcoming tired and thirsty travelers since it was first built in 1773, and today it combines the charm of the Colonial era with the amenities required by the current generations of pilgrims. The present have lovingly restored the old Inn with period antiques and authentic materials. It has a fine restaurant which offers nightly entertainment in addition to traditional American cuisine. Jac and Jane Fitzpatrick, who saved the Red Lion from being torn down and replaced by a gas station a few years back, also own Country Curtains, the first mail order curtain company, which they started more than twenty-five years ago. If you write to them at the above address, they'll send you a catalogue.

Plymouth

Plymouth alone can rival Boston's claim as the New England community boasting the most historic past. And while the larger city is clearly the place to explore the Revolutionary Period, Plymouth, as the site of the first settlement in the northern colonies, is held in reverence by most Americans as a symbol of the triumphant spirit of our early ancestors. The initial party of Pilgrims met with tragedy here when half of them died of scurvy and other illnesses during the winter of 1620-1621. By the following fall, however, the colony had been replenished by new arrivals and was strong enough to celebrate the first Thanksgiving, along with about twenty friendly Indian guests.

What to See

Mayflower II, State Pier on Water Street. In an effort to learn about life for the 102 passengers and 25 crewmen during the initial crossing, a 33-man crew sailed across from England in 1957 in this full scale replica of the original *Mayflower*. The ship is now the site of displays and demonstrations of maritime activities and skills of the early 1600s. Open daily 9-5 between April and November. Admission $1.75 for adults; $1.25 for children.

Plymouth Rock, Water Street. No one really knows for sure if this is where the first settlers landed but the cracked stone with 1620 carved into the top that sits on this spot has burrowed its was deep into the mythology and consciousness of the American people. The rock itself is quite small, and is protected by bars and a granite canopy designed in 1880.

Jabez Howland House, 33 Sandwich Street. Built in 1667 by the son of one of the original settlers, the residence is now a museum owned by the Pilgrim Howland Society. It has displays of textiles, period antiques, and farm implements. Open May 25-July, Sa, Su 10-5; July 2-September 14, daily, 10-5; September 16-October 12, Sa, Su 10-5; October 13-Thanksgiving, Su 12-5. Admission is $1.25 for adults; 50¢ for children.

Plymouth Antiquarian Society. Three houses operated by this orgainization are among Plymouth's most popular attractions. The 1809 Federal-style *Antiquarian House*, 126 Water Street, has a beautiful collection of Lowestoft, Canton, and Staffordshire ware. *Harlow Old Fort House*, 119 Sandwich Street, has a unique history. After King Philip's War, the first Pilgrim fort was torn down and the beams given to Sargeant William Harlow who used them to build this dwelling. Women in period dress offer demonstrations of Colonial crafts such as spinning and weaving here. The *Spooner House*, 27 North Street, was the home of the Spooner family for more than two hundred years. Today the building is a museum with an extraordinary variety of heirlooms, thanks to the generosity of James Spooner, the family scion who bequeathed the house to the public upon his death in 1954. All three of these houses are open May 27-September 15, Th-Sa 10-5, Su 10-5.

Richard Sparrow House, 42 Summer Street. Built in 1640, the oldest Plymouth residence still standing is home to the Plymouth Potter Guild. The house belonged first to Richard Sparrow and his wife, who arrived at the settlement twelve years after the initial group of immigrants. After 1651, their son, Jonathan, became the owner. Though parts of the house were enlarged over the years, it was restored in the 1930s and still retains its original floorboards and fireplace. Open May 15-October 15, Mo-Sa 9-5. Admission is $1.25 adults; 25¢ children.

The Mayflower Society House, 4 Winslow Street. Built in 1704 as the residence of Edward Winslow, this home is now administered by the General Society of Mayflower Descendants, hence the name. Winslow, a Tory, abandoned the colony during the Revolution because of his unpopular views. Saved from being torn down to make way for a parking lot in 1941, the nine-room building today houses resplendant antique furniture from the 1600s to 1800s. Open daily from May 30-October 15 9-5. Admission is $1.25 for adults; 25¢ for children.

Plymouth Plantation, Warren Road, three miles south of downtown. Conceived in 1947, this complex is a full-scale reproduction that parallels as much as possible the architecture, dress, and daily activities of the first settlers. "Villagers" in authentic period outfits perform the day-to-day agricultural, domestic, and cultural activites common in the settlement. They also answer questions from visitors. Nearby is the *Wampanoag Summer Settlement*, created just a couple of years ago. Staffed by native American Indians, it serves as an ideal complement to the Pilgrim village by depicting the everyday routine of the Indians who first befriended the English arrivals. Both settlements are open from May 1 to October 31, 9-5 daily. Admission is $4.50 for adults; $2.25 for children.

Where to Stay

The Colonial House Inn, 207 Sandwich Street, Plymouth, MA 02360. Tel: (617) 746-2087. Six rooms, all with private bath. Doubles run $55 a day. Reservations should be made a month in advance. Onwers: Oscar and Olga Isaacs.

A most charming little inn decorated with Colonial period pieces, the Colonial House is located near all the major sites in Plymouth. No restaurant.

Where to Shop

Gordon and Genevieve Deming, 125 Wadsworth Road, Duxbury, MA 02332. Tel: (617) 934-5259. Appointments advisable. Gordon and Genevieve Deming. This shop, in business for more than fifteen years, features Early American furniture, primitives, oils, pewter, tools, fireplace items, and stoneware. Prices range from $5 to $10,000.

Springfield, Deerfield, & Amherst _____

Springfield gained prominence during the 19th century as one of the leading commercial towns in western Massachusetts. From 1794 until 1964, the Federal Armory here was an important symbol of Springfield's industrial might; when it finally closed, it was a clear indication that the community had fallen on hard economic times. It remains, however, a highlight of any exploration of New England's cultural, historic, and architectural traditions. To the north lies one of the most distinguished academic centers in the country. Amherst, home of Amherst College and the University of Massachusetts (with Smith, Mount Holyoke, and Hampshire Colleges all within easy commuting distance) maintains a literary and scholarly reputation as renowned today as it has been for the past two hundred years. Deerfield, site of the superb preparatory school Deerfield Academy, has perhaps the strongest sense of history of the three communities. Indeed, the locals still remember the stories of the 1675 and 1704 massacres, when the town was twice nearly decimated by Indian attacks.

What to See

Springfield Armory National Historic Site, Armory Square, is an ideal place for military buffs to start a tour of the region. The building houses the finest collection of small arms in the world. The site of the Armory was selected by George Washington himself, and the town's gunsmiths quickly gained widespread fame as among the nation's best. Open daily 8-4:30. Admission is free.

Ames Hill-Crescent Hill Historic District. Located in an area circumscribed by Central, Maple, Mill, and Pine Street, Crescent Hill, Ames Hill Drive and Maple Court, this district offers a fine view of the residential architectural styles popular among the rich from the 1820s to the 1930s. Of particular interest are the *Mills-Stebbins Villa*, a two-story brick dwelling in the Italian villa style with a loggia within a three-story square tower; the Queen Anne style *Walter Wesson House*, with turrets and a facade of brownstone, brick, and shingling;

and the white brick *David Ames House*, combining elements of both Federal and Greek Revival styles.

Court Square Historic District. Springfield's key municipal buildings are located around the lovely common known as *Court Square Park* and within an area defined by Main, State, and Pynchon Streets, Broadway and City Hall Place. The oldest building here is Isaac Damon's neo-classical *First Church of Christ*, built in 1819. Henry Hobston Richardson designed the granite Romanesque *Hampden County Courthouse*, graced with tall, elegant entry arches. Nearby, a 300-foot camponile provides a spectacular view of the Connecticut River Valley, and the renovated Auditorium boasts a capacity of 4,000. East of Court Square is the *Connecticut Valley Historical Museum*, 194 State Street, home of archives and documents spanning three centuries, period rooms and exhibits on decorative and practical arts. Open Tu 12-9, We-Su 2-5. Admission is free.

Any visit to *Amherst* must start on the Common, the site of the *Amherst College Campus* since 1821. The school, with its Georgian Colonial red brick buildings--together with Williams College in western Massachusetts and Weleyan College in central Connecticut--comprise what is called today the "Little Ivy League."

Nehemiah Strong House, 67 Amity Street, is Amherst's oldest. Built in 1744, the clapboard and frame dwelling now houses relics and furniture dating back to the 18th century. Memorial Day-Labor Day Tu, Th-Fr 1-4.

Emily Dickinson Home, 280 Main Street. Amherst's most famous house is known not for its elegance or style but for being the home of the city's most illustrious resident--poet Emily Dickinson. Ironically, though she lived in a community teeming with new students every year, this Amherst native composed her astonishing verse as a virtual recluse, particularly in the latter years of her life. The house is open for tours scheduled by appointment on Tu and Fr at 1:45, 3, and 4:30. Arrange by calling (413) 542-2321.

Dickinson Historic District. The poet's home, a Federal structure built in 1813, is in the heart of this district bounded by Tayler Place and Main, Lessey and Triangle Streets. Most of the other houses in the district were constructed later in mid-century and incorporate Italianate and Italian villa architectural details. Two excellent examples are the *William Aus-*

tin Dickinson House, 214 Main Street, commissioned in the 1850s by Emily's father, and the twin *Hills Houses*, 360 Main Street, owned by Leonard Hills, the guiding light behind the creation of the Massachusetts Agricultural College, later to become the Amherst branch of the University of Massachusetts.

All visitors to *Deerfield* quickly find The Street, formerly called Old Deerfield Street. Along the walkway lies *Historic Deerfield*, an enclave of twelve historic buildings--a non-profit celebration of the town's past established in 1952 by residents Harry and Helen Flynt. The obvious care with which these buildings have been restored is indicative of the town pride which has ensured that Deerfield is among the best preserved of New England's Colonial and 19th century communities.

The oldest of the houses on view in Historic Deerfield--the only one, in fact, built at least in part before the 1704 massacre--is the *Frary House*. Located on the town common, it served at one time as a tavern and became an important Whig meeting place during the Revolutionary years. The house, restored in 1890, contains a splendid 19th century ballroom and examples of period decorative arts. The *Asa Stebbins House* is a late Georgian Colonial brick residence dating from the turn of the 19th century. The interior, with French wallpaper, fine rugs, extensive wall paintings, and elegant period furniture, reflects the wealth of the Stebbins family. Indeed, in 1824, Stebbins built a second dwelling for his son and namesake. Superb Chippendale and Adam furnishings, along with tea sets from the early days of the China trade, grace this Federal period. Antiques owned by Caleb Strong, an early Massachusetts governor, are also on display.

The *Allen House*, a saltbox dwelling with a center chimney, dates from the same period. In the current century, it became the home of Historic Deerfield founder Harry and Helen Flynt, and it still contains their lavish collection of beautiful antique furniture, needlework, and domestic artifacts common in the 1800s. A converted barn is today the location of the *Helen Geier Flynt Fabric Hall*. A must for anyone interested in the history of needlework, costumes, and textiles, the exhibits offer samples from America, England, and Europe spanning three centuries. Nearby is the *Parker and Russell Silver Shop*, housed in an 1814 farmhouse. Revere,

Dummer, Coney, and Mayers are among the artisans repre-
sented in its superb display of American and English silver.
The shop also boasts a standard silversmith's workshop and a
country parlor from the Federal period.

Historic Deerfield also contains a number of structures
transported to the complex from elsewhere. The *Wilson Printing Shop* has served as a grocery, home, and book bindery in
seven different locations around town. A hand press and a
variety of printed documents dating from the late 1700s are
the treasures on display in this 1816 frame building. The
Dwight Barnard House was originally built in Springfield in
1725, and was removed to Deerfield in the early 1950s to
complement the other Historic Deerfield structures. Seven
chambers in this impressive early Georgian Colonial home,
including a kitchen, parlor, bedroom with elegant grained
paneling, and an 18th century doctor's office, have been
fleshed out with distinctive period furniture. The *Ashley
House*, built around 1730, has been returned to its original
location and restored with scrupulous attention to detail. During the Revolutionary period, it was the home of the town's
Reverend Ashley, a staunch supporter of the British despite
the refusal of his angry parishioners to pay the Tory clergyman
his wages.

The *Historic Deerfield* buildings are open year-round
Mo-Sa 9:30-4:30, Su 1-4:30. Admission for each averages $1.50
for adults; 50¢ for children. Combination fee for three buildings is $3.50; $12 for eleven buildings. For information on
special lectures, tours, and other events write Historic Deerfield, Box 321, Deerfield, MA 01342, or call (413) 773-8689.

Other Deerfield Sights. While Historic Deerfield is the
town's major attraction for collectors, there are several other
places worth seeing. *Memorial Hall*, designed in 1798 as the
first of Deerfield Academy's buildings, has been a museum
devoted to the history of the region since 1880. The highlight
of the exhibit is a door from a house built in 1698. It's called
the "Indian House Door," thanks to its historic importance as
a heavily damaged, but still intact, survivor of the Indian massacre of 1704. Implements and tools crucial to life in Colonial
times are on display in a kitchen, parlor, and bedroom; these
room are the nation's oldest period reproductions. Located on
Memorial Street, the museum is open from May 1-October 31

Mo-Fr 10-4:30, Sa-Su 12:30-4:30; by appointment April and
November. Admission is $1.50 adults; $1 students; 50¢ children. Family rate is $3.50. For information, call (413) 773-
8929.

The *Indian House Memorial* and *Bloody Brook Tavern*,
side by side on The Street, feature antique furniture, decorative objects, and spinning artifacts. Open May 1-October 31
Mo, We, Sa, 1-5; Su, holidays 9:30-12 and 1-4. Admission is
$1.50 adults; $1 students; 50¢ children.

Where to Stay

The Deerfield Inn, The Street, Deerfield, MA 01342.
Tel: (413) 774-5587. Twenty-three rooms; the Inn also makes
reservation for rooms available in homes down The Street.
Daily rates for all are $65 and $70 for singles or doubles.
General manager: Paul Burns.

Located at the mid-point of The Street, Deerfield's central mile-long walkway, the Inn is just a few minutes walk
from any of the twelve historic homes comprising Historic
Deerfield, as well as the other town sites. Originally built in
1884, the Inn has been expanded a number of times since.
Boasting a decor and furnishings that recall the easy grace of
19th century New England life, the Inn also includes an elegant dining room with capacity of eighty-five people, two
cocktail lounges for mid-afternoon and early-evening relaxa-
tion, a coffee shop, and a series of private meeting rooms for
special events.

Where to Shop

In Amherst:

R and R French, Antiques, 657 South Pleasant Street,
Amherst, MA 01002. Tel: (413) 253-2269. Open 9-5 Mo-Sa.
Rachel C. French. In business for forty-five years. Sells "arti-
cles over one hundred years old."

The Wood-Shed Antiques, 156 Montague Road, Rte. 63,
Amherst, MA 01002. Tel: (413) 549-1720. Open daily except
weekends. Beatrice and Harlan Wood, Jr. In business thirty-
three years, the Wood-Shed offers china, glass, iron, tin, and
wooden primitives. Prices range from $1 up.

In Greenfield:

Red Barn of Greenfield, 95 River Street, Greenfield, MA 01301. Tel: (413) 773-7225. Open 9-5 Mo-Sa. Howard J. Arkush. This twenty-year-old shop offers 18th and 19th century furniture, some glass, paintings, bric-a-brac, and so on.

In Hadley:

Antiques 'n Oddities Too, 229 Russell Street, Rte. 9, Hadley, MA 01035. Tel: (413) 253-7646. Open 10-5 daily, closed We. Rich and Flo Newman. Specializes in wood carvings, musical instruments, much unusual and eclectic furniture. Prices run from $7.50 to $750.

Hadley Antiques Center, 227 Russell Street, Rte. 9, Hadley, MA 01035. Tel: (413) 586-4093. Open 10-5 daily, closed We. Ted and Sue Allen, owners. This cooperative shop of more than thirty-five dealers offers a wide range of merchandise: Golden Oak to primitive furniture, country store advertising, linens, quilts, books, ephemera, all periods glass and china. Prices range from $1 to $1,000.

Metamorphosis, 206 Russell Street, Hadley, MA 01035. Tel: (413) 584-8810. Open 10-5:30, Tu-Sa. Anne and Bob Berra. Antique furniture and accessories. Prices run from $1 to $1,000, mostly in the $10 to $500 range.

In Northampton:

White Star Gallery, 46 Green Street, Northampton, MA 01060. Tel: (413) 586-3166. Irregular hours. Charles E. Derby. White Star Gallery specializes in antique American Indian, African, and Oceanic art. Prices range from $5 to $10,000.

In South Deerfield:

Lighthouse Antiques, Rte. 5-10, South Deerfield, MA 01373. Tel: (413) 665-2488. Open daily 9-5. Edward S. Petrovic. In business fifteen years. All antiques, no collectibles. Prices from $1 to $5,000.

In Springfield:

Springfield Antique Center, 100 Boston Road, Springfield, MA 01109. Tel: (413) 736-2388. Open 10-5 Tu-Sa, Su 12-5. Bill and Nancy Bakeman, Jeff and Judy Browne. This shop, fifteen years in buisess, features 18th and 19th century furniture and accessories. Prices run from $5 to $1,000 and more.

Worcester & Environs _____

Worcester is located in the central Massachusetts countryside amidst a setting of gentle hills, small valleys and reservoirs, and the Deerfield and Connecticut River Valleys. With a host of renowned cultural institutions, the town itself remains an intellectural and artistic center. In the 19th century, Worcester's emergence as an important industrial city provided entrepreneurs with a vital opportunity to amass family fortunes. The descendants of some of those early tycoons are among the area's leading citizens today. While Worcester has seen some hard economic times in recent years, the strong community spirit is evident from the successful recent efforts to reclaim and renovate the downtown area.

What to See

The American Antiquarian Society, 185 Salisbury Street, is one of the country's leading research institutions, second only perhaps to the Library of Congress in Washington, D.C. Founded in 1812, it moved to its current location in 1910. The Society is particulary famous for its collections of Early American newspapers and fiction, as well as the rest of the 650,000 volumes of original source material covering the American experience up until 1877. Visitors can attend lectures, tours, and exhibitions. Open Mo-Fr 9-5. No charge.

The Worcester Historical Museum, 39 Salisbury Street, is noted for its displays of costumes and military paraphernalia, as well as other historical objects. Open Tu-Sa 1-4. Admission is free.

Mechanics Hall, 321 Main Street, a Renaissance revival structure with a brick and iron facade, was the scene in the 1800s of presentations by many of the era's greatest speakers, performers, and artists. It is one of the many buildings restored during the recent downtown revival.

The Timothy Paine House, 140 Lincoln Street, is, ironically, now under the care of the local chapter of the Daughters of the American Revolution. Ironic, indeed, since Paine was an ardent Tory. Of special interest are the slate and marble fireplaces and 18th century furniture. Open by appointment only. For information, write to The Colonel Timothy Bigelow Chapter of the Daughters of the American Revolution, Timothy Paine House, 140 Lincoln Street, Worcester, MA 01605.

Three more buildings of historic interest were constructed by members of the Salisbury family, one of Worcester's most distinguished. In the late 18th century, Bostonian Stephen Salisbury launched a local hardware business and built the *Salisbury Mansion and Store* at 30 and 40 Highland Street. Both are two-story clapboard structures with elegant architectural details--the mansion with its neo-classical portico and exquisite woodwork, and the store with its central Palladian window on the second floor. *The Salisbury House*, 61 Harvard Street, was built in 1836 by Stephen Salisbury, Jr. Spacious rooms and a spiral staircase grace the interior of this Greek Revival residence.

Worcester Environs. The town's around Worcester offer the adventurous traveler a number of unexpected delights. In Grafton, the talent and ingenuity of the Willard family is commemorated in the *Willard House and Clock Museum*, on Willard Street. Benjamin, Simon, Ephraim, and Aaron Willard were among the area's preeminent timepiece makers from the 1770s well into the 1800s. The building houses not only watches and clocks but also tools, portraits, and other family memorabilia. Open Tu-Sa 10-4, Su 1-5, holidays 1-4. Admission is $1.50 for adults; 75¢ for children.

In Harvard, one mile south of MA 2A on Shaker Road, are the remains of *Harvard Shaker Village*, founded in the 1790s. At its peak in the 1820s, nearly two hundred members lived and farmed on the community's 1800 acres. The experiment came to an end, however, in 1918 and today only a handful of the buildings are still standing; among them are the meeting house, the tailor shop, and an administration headquarters. Some of the crafts, furnishings, and other objects from the Village can be found in the nearby *Fruitlands Museum* on Prospect Hill Road. Fruitlands was the site, in 1843 and 1844, of a communal society called New Eden. Founded by philospher Bronson Alcott, father of author Louisa May, it captivated the imaginations and captured the endorsements of such leading lights of the Transcendental Movement as Emerson, Thoreau, and Margaret Fuller. New Eden could not survive, however, largely because members were forbidden to profit from or exploit the labor of any other human being or animal. The headquarters was in the *Farmstead*, built around 1750. Also on the grounds are the *American Indian Museum* and *Picture Gallery* with a large collection of work of the Hudson River School painters.

With over one hundred buildings, *Old Sturbridge Village*, located where the MA Tpk, I-86, US 20, and MA 131 meet, is an impressive and accurate reproduction of a rural Massachusetts town from the first half of the 19th century. Many of the buildings were transported to Sturbridge from elsewhere in the region. These include the *Harvey Brooks Pottery Shop*, a Connecticut structure from the early 1800s which features a display of a potter's essential equipment; the *Asa Knight General Store*, an 1811 Vermont building whose shelves are now stocked with samples of period goods; the *Isaiah Thomas Printing Office,* transported from Worcester, where in the early Federal period it was owned by one of the nation's most important publishers; and the *Thomas Bank,* an 1835 Greek Revival structure from Connecticut that serves as a reminder of the growing importance of the banking industry in the economic life of New England towns of the time. *Sturbridge* is open from April 1-October 24 daily 9:30-5:30 and from October 25-March 30 Mo-Fr 1-4, Sa-Su 9:30-4:30. Admission for all buildings is $7 for adults; $3 for children ages six to fifteen; under six free.

Where to Shop

Brimfield Antiques, Haynes Hill Road, Brimfield, MA 01010. Tel: (413) 245-3350. Open by appointment. Richard and Susan Raymond. Near Old Sturbridge Village, the Raymonds specilize in American furniture before 1840. Prices are in a full range.

New Hampshire

Conway●

Center Sandwich●

●Hanover

●Cornish

●Laconia

● Concord
●Hopkinton
Henniker ●
Hillsboro ●
Newington
Portsmouth
Keene ●Hancock ●Manchester
Marlborough ●Bedford
W. Swanzey ●Peterborough
●Fitzwilliam

First settled in Portsmouth in 1623, New Hampshire was administered as part of Massachusetts until 1679 when it became a royal colony. Fierce supporters of the Revolution, the New Hampshire Colony declared its independence from Great Britain seven months before the Declaration of Independence on July 4, 1776. Colonel John Stark's heroic words "Live free or die" are the state's motto.

The White Mountains, tallest in New England, are the major tourist attraction, bringing in skiers and hikers in droves. With 1,300 lakes and 1,500 miles of streams, New Hampshire is also a fisherman's paradise, offering trout, salmon, bass, and other lively game fish for the taking.

For the collector, New Hampshire's primary attractions are Portsmouth, with its many fine historic homes, and its restored "Strawbery Banke" settlement and the magnificently maintained Saint-Gaudens National Historic Site in Cornish, a memorial to the most famous sculptor of the of the 19th century.

Center Sandwich, Conway, & Laconia

Three of the prettiest of all New England villages, Laconia rests on the southern edge of Lake Winnipesaukee and Center Sandwich just to the lake's north; still further upland is Conway on the border of the White Mountain National Forest and Mt. Washington. Center Sandwich is an especially picturesque village with its white clapboard houses and green rolling hills. It also offers the best shopping. Conway has a fine inn and Laconia is home to the best roast duckling in all of New England.

What to See

Elisha Marston House, Maple Street, Center Sandwich. An 1850 building, this is the home of the Sandwich Historical Society which maintains an excellent collection of paintings, farm implements, and furniture. Craft displays are regularly featured. Open Mo-Sa 11-5 in July and August; 2-5 June and September. Free.

Scenic Railroads. The visitor to northern New Hampshire has a choice of two great railway rides. Most famous is the *Mount Washington Cog Railway*. Built in 1869, this three and one-half mile route offers a scary ride to the summit aboard a small steam-operated train, which must surmount grades as steep as 37 percent. The other choice is the *Conway Scenic Railroad*, which departs from a Russian-style station built in North Conway in 1874. It offers an eleven mile ride through the Saco River valley. Heaven for railroad buffs.

Hickory Stick Farm, RFD 2, Bean Hill Road, Laconia, NH 03246. The attraction here is food--specifically roast duckling. This small country restaurant was opened by Charlie and Dee Roeder in 1950 when they converted their charming set of colonial farm buildings and began concentrating on serving great meals in an Early American atmosphere. Their son Scott and his wife Mary have continued the tradition. Open from Memorial Day to Columbus Day, dinner is served from 5-9 every night and noon-9 on Su. Incidentally, the Roeders also have a couple of guest rooms which they rent for $42 to $48, including breakfast. Don't miss their fine collection of antiques--after you've finished eating.

Where to Stay

Darby Field Inn, Bald Hill Road, Conway, NH 03818. Tel: (603) 447-2181 or 447-2198. Seventeen rooms, fifteen baths. Open January 1 thru March 26; April 29 thru October 29; November 18 thru December 31. Rooms are designed ideally for double occupancy; $50 to $70. Children aged two to twelve sharing a room with parents $25. Innkeepers: Marc and Marily Donaldson.

This charming country retreat with its spectacular views of Mt. Washington and the White Mountains was first settled in 1826 by Samuel and Polly Chase Littlefield and remained in the family for many years. In the 1940s, a Boston florist named Abraham Covin moved his family here and created The Bald Hill Lodge, turning the original farmhouse into the living room section of the inn and replacing the barn and blacksmith's shop with a dining room and kitchen. Marc Donaldson and his Venezuelan-born wife Marily arrived in the spring of 1979 and created the current ambiance which is highlighted by gourmet cooking. Rooms are very comfortable and individually decorated. A delightful place to sit in front of the huge fireplace or to watch the sunset from the dining room.

Where to Shop

In Center Sandwich:

Ayotte's Designery, Maple Street, Center Sandwich, NH 03227. Tel: (603) 284-6915. Open 10-5 Th-Sa. Robert and Roberta Ayotte. In business for over twenty-five years, the Ayottes design and handweave a full line of original clothing (capes, coats, tops, skirts, dresses, ponchos, and so on), rugs, wall hangings, tapestries, and gift items. Prices range from 50¢ to $300.

Sunshine Farm - Congdon and Co., Rte. 113 E, Center Sandwich, NH 03227. Tel: (603) 284-6400. Open 9-5 by chance or by appointment. Arthur S. Congdon, Jr. General line of American antiques. Prices run from $10 to $2,000 and up.

In Laconia:

Hoffman's 1780 Cape Antiques, Box 434, RD 2, Laconia, NH 03246. Tel: (603) 528-2792. Open by chance or by appointment; call ahead. George and Gloria Hoffman. The Hoffmans feature primitive Americana, furniture and accessories, cupboards, country furniture, early iron, pewter, paintings, baskets, quilts, crocks, pantry boxes, firkings, and "everything for the country kitchen." Prices range from $5 to $4,000, most are below $1,000.

Concord & Environs

Although fewer than 30,000 people reside in New Hampshire's capital city, Concord has an influence beyond its size. The largest state legislature in the nation (424 representatives) is located here, a local attorney became the only man from New Hampshire ever to be elected President, and the Concord coach--manufactured here by the Abbot-Downing Company during the 19th century--is widely remembered as the "wagon that won the west." Situated along a bend in the Merrimack River, this central New Hampshire town boasts some interesting architecture and is today the transportation and commercial center of the state.

What to See

Concord Historic District. One of the earliest residential areas of town, this district boasts some splendid examples of a number of architectural styles in structures built between the 1730s to the mid-20th century. Oldest among them is the *Reverend Timothy Walker House*, 276 North Main Street. Built around 1733 by the city's first minister, a man who packed a gun even when in the pulpit to ward off Indians, this is a fine example of the Georgian style. With its gambrel roof and classic details, the house is related to houses of the same period in coastal towns like Portsmouth. Just next door at 278 North Main Street is the *Joseph B. Walker Cottage*, a splendid Gothic Revival house based on a design by architect Andrew Jackson Downing. The most famous house in the district is the *Pierce Manse*, 14 Penacook Street, home of Franklin Pierce, 14th President of the U.S. and a Concord native. Unfortunately, the house and much of its memorabilia were damaged by fire a few years back. While in the district, you'll want to visit the *New Hampshire League of Craftsmen* headquarters at 205 North Main Street and their main sales shop at 136 North Main Street. The League has been in business more than fifty years, has 3,000 members and ten retail shops around the state, and features handcrafted glass, textiles, silver, wood, and pottery items. The sales shop is open 10-5 daily, except Su.

New Hampshire Historical Society and Library, 30 Park Street. A handsome granite building designed by Boston architect Guy Lowell, the Society houses a rare collection of artifacts and records on New Hampshire's history. The front entrance is dominated by a massive statue called "Ancient and Modern History" carved from local granite by Daniel Chester French. A restored 1853 Concord coach is located on the ground floor. On the second floor, you can see the 1780 Chippendale slant-top desk that Franklin Pierce used in his local law office. the Prentis Collection--housed in four 18th century period rooms--is a splendid gathering of antiques and portraits that recreate the home style of a wealthy Colonial merchant. Open 9-4:30 Mo-Fr. Admission is free.

The State House 25 State Street. This is the oldest state capitol where the legislature still meets in its original chambers. See the Barry Faulkner murals in the Senate Chamber that depict scenes from the state's history. On the grounds, you'll find statues of famous native sons Daniel Webster, Franklin Pierce, and Colonel John Stark.

Franklin Pierce Homestead, NH 9, twenty-two miles west of Concord. This small, clapboard frame house built in 1804 is a superb example of Federal architecture. The original home of the 14th President, the house has some fine French wallpaper and a ballroom. Open late June through Labor Day, Tu-Su 9-5. On the drive out, you'll want to stop and see the *Henniker Covered Bridge*, fifteen miles west of Concord.

Where to Stay

The John Hancock Inn, Main Street, Hancock, NH 03449. Tel: (603) 525-3318. Ten rooms, all with private baths. Doubles run $46.50 a night; singles $39.50. Reservations should be made as far in advance as possible. Owners: Glynn and Pat Wells.

This famous old inn has been in business since 1789 and under the direction of the Wells since 1973. Its original gable roof was replaced by a mansard in the mid-1850s, its first and second story porches by tall columns and a new first floor porch in this century. The carriage lounge has tables made from bellows and seats from old buggies. The lobby is reminiscent of a country store. There are three dining rooms open for breakfast, lunch, and dinner for guests and travelers alike, featuring hearty New England cuisine. The inn is furnished with antiques and reproductions (handmade by local craftsmen). There are handmade braided and hooked rugs, old bed-steads and cabinets, print, and engravings. In one room, the walls are painted with murals by Rufus Porter. In the chambermaid's room are the remains of stenciled designs by Moses Eaton, who lived nearby. A delight.

Where to Shop

In Concord:
F.E. Hamel Antiques, 150 Loudon Road, Concord, NH 03301. Tel: (603) 224-7949. Open daily 10-5. F.E. Hamel. Specialist in pocket watches and small items. Prices range from $5 to $2,000.

In Hancock:
Hardings of Hancock, Depot Street, Bos 65, Hancock, NH 03449. Tel: (603) 525-3518. Open by chance or by appointment. Lee and Vince Harding. This nineteen-year-old shop features early lighting, iron, tin, woodware, brass, copper, country furniture, primitive accents. Prices from $10 to $2,000.

Sand Pond Shops, Shady Lane, Hancock, NH 03449. Tel: (603) 525-6615. Open by appointment. James C. Tillinghast. In business for twenty years, Sand Pond offers antique ammunition, tins, bottles, tools, paper Americana, country store items. Prices run from 50¢ to $500.

In Hillsboro:
Black Sheep Antiques, East Washington Road, Hillsboro, NH 03244. Tel: (603) 478-5749. Open 10-5 Most days; call to be sure. Ellen and Russ Heston. Country furniture, kitchenware and lamps, handcrafted shades made to order. Prices from $1 to $1,000.

Country Collector Antiques Barn, School Street, off Rtes. 202 and 9, Hillsboro, NH 03244. Tel: (603) 464-5200. Open by chance or by appointment, usually 11-5. Features old oil lamps; also primitives, iron, wood, tools, glass, and furniture. Prices from $1 to $500.

Old Dunbar House, Centre Road, Hillsboro Centre, NH 03244. Tel: (603) 464-3937. Open daily by appointment. Ralph C. Stuart. This forty-year-old shop offers "nothing after

1830." Porcelain, pewter, and American furniture. Prices are $100 and up; mostly up.

Well Sweep Antiques, Hillsboro Centre, Hillsboro, NH 03244. Tel: (603) 464-3218. Open by chance or by appointment. Richard W. Withington, Jr. Early country furniture and decorative accessories. Prices run from $25 to $2,000.

In Hopkinton:

Finder's Keepers, Hopkinton Road, Rtes. 202 and 9, Hopkinton, NH 03301. Tel: (603) 224-4412. Open daily 10-6 May to November. Thelma H. McIntosh. Offers antique clothes, linens, country store items, books, postcards and ephemera, china, glass, furniture, old and interesting collectibles.

Hanover

A pretty colonial town on the banks of the Connecticut River, Hanover is the home of Dartmouth College, one of the premier Ivy League schools. Founded in 1769 by the Reverend Eleazar Wheelock "for the education of youth of the Indian tribes" and for "English youth and others," Dartmouth's distinguished alumni include Daniel Webster and Nelson A. Rockefeller, among many others. Hanover is a college town, pure and simple, with ivy-covered buildings, walkways shaded by giant maples and elms, and pretty white frame houses.

What to See

Dartmouth Row. This group of four white brick buildings is located on the site where Reverend Wheelock dug the first well for his aspiring instituion. In the center is *Dartmouth Hall*, a replica of the original 1784 structure that burned down in 1904. The Row overlooks *The Green*, a seven-and-a-half acre clearing carved from the towering white pines in the 1830s.

Baker Memorial Library. Located just to the north of The Green, Baker Library is modeled after Independence Hall in Philadelphia. With its 200-foot tower, this massive home of more than one million books is hard to miss. For art lovers, the attraction is the 3,000-square-foot mural called "An Epic of American Civilization" which fills the walls of the basement reading room. Painted by Mexican artist Jose Clemente Orozco in 1932-34, these magnificent frescoes have as their theme nothing less than the 5,000 year history of the Americas. The library is open from 8 in the morning until midnight.

Where to Shop

League of New Hampshire Craftsmen, 13 Lebanon Street, Hanover, NH 03755. Tel: (603) 643-5050. Open daily 9:30-5. In business for more than fifty years, the League offers crafts in a broad price range.

Keene & Environs

In the 19th and early 20th centuries, Keene--and the neighboring town of Stoddard--were important pottery and glassworks centers and staples of the New Hampshire economy. The area has continued as a commercial center but its factories today produce more prosaic items like shoes, tools, textiles, and furniture. For the collector, however, the area has a number of surprising treats.

What to See

Colony House Museum, 104 West Street. Housed in the 1817 Federal mansion of Horatio Colony, Keene's first mayor, are outstanding collections of glass from the first glass factories in the nation and Hampshire Pottery which was produced in Keene between 1871 and 1923. Also featured are manuscripts and documents from the Revolutionary period bearing the signatures of such notables as John Hancock, George Washington, and Thomas Jefferson. Early Colonial silver includes an exceptionally rare tankard, a porringer, and a Paul Revere spoon. From the era of glass manufacturing, which flourished in Keene and Stoddard between 1814 and 1873, are choice examples of blown decanters, flasks, bitters, ink and bottles, as well as "end of the day" souvenir pieces. There's also a magnificent collection of old Staffordshire china, part of which was brought down the Connecticut River by boat from Canada during the early 1800s. On the second floor of the museum is a collection of the famed Kingsbury iron toys made in Keene. All this is topped off by a unique collection of miniature wood turnings, some dolls, and Civil War relics. Open Tu-Su 10-4:30 from May 1 to October 12. Admission is $1; children under twelve free.

The Wyman Tavern, 339 Main Street. Built in 1762 by Captain Isaac Wyman, a verteran of the Indian wars, "Keene's Most Historic House" is a large frame structure. It was from here that Wyman led twenty-nine Minutemen on the march to Lexington on the morning of April 21, 1775. Even before that, on October 22, 1770, to be precise, the trustees of Dartmouth College held their first meeting here, an event commemorated by the trustees of the college in 1970 when they convened in the same room where their predecessors first met. The tavern is now a museum, housing collections of antiques, books, and portraits. Open Tu-Th 1-4 from June to October. Donations are accepted.

The Game Preserve, 110 Spring Road, Peterborough. Owned by Lee and Rally Dennis, this private museum of antique board and card games is a fascinating detour for collectors. Over seven hundred and fifty old board and card games are on display in this unique collection. Games dating back to 1820 include the first board game manufactured in America. This may be the only place in the world where you can play the Colonial game of skittles or engage in a rousing round of tenpin. Duplicates from the collection are for sale, as well as other unusual items, on the museum's Pastime Porch. Open year-round by chance or appointment. Tel: (603) 924-6710. Admission is $1.50 for adults; $1 for children.

Where to Stay

Fitzwilliam Inn, Rte. 119, Fitzwilliam, NH 03447. Tel: (603) 585-9000. Twenty-five rooms; fifteen baths. Reservations should be made several weeks in advance. Doubles range from $26 to $30. Owners: Barbara and Charles Wallace.

This old-fashioned New England country inn has been welcoming weary-travelers continuously since 1796, ten years under the capable hands of the Wallaces. Located fourteen miles south of Keene, the Inn is ideally situated for exploring southern New Hampshire. There is a restaurant featuring traditional New England fare. Exceptionally good value. Nice wine list.

Where to Shop

In Fitzwilliam:

Bloomin Antiques, Box 642, Fitzwilliam, NH 03447. Tel: (603) 585-9092. Mark O. Sipson. Period furniture and accessories. Prices run from $5 to $2,500.

William Lewan Antiques, Old Troy Road, Fitzwilliam, NH 03447. Tel: (603) 585-3365. Open daily 10-5. William Lewan. Country furniture and accessories.

In Keene:

Beech Hill Gallery, Concord Road, Keene, NH 03431. Tel: (603) 352-2194. Open 9-5 by appointment. Harold A. Goder. This fifteen-year-old shop sells silver, paintings, quilts, furniture. Prices from $10 to $3,500.

Betty Willis Antiques, 100 Washington St., Keene, NH 03431. Tel: (603) 352-5929. Open every day except Mo. Betty W. Barenholtz. In business for over twenty years, this shop offers American country and semi-formal furniture and accessories.

Dale Pregent Antiques, 142 Marboro Street, Keene, NH 03431. Tel: (603) 352-6736. Open by chance or by appointment. Dale Pregent. In business for more than fifteen years. Stoneware, dolls, banks, toys, pewter, Currier and Ives prints, fire related items.

Lillian Wiener, 695 Court Street, Keene, NH 03431. Tel: (603) 352-8215. Open by chance or by appointment. Lillian Wiener. Primitive, country and decorative (continental) accessories; emphasis on unusual kitchen accessories. Prices run from $25 to $3,000.

Tavern Antiques and Baseball Memorabilia, Keene, NH 03431. Tel: (603) 352-0054. Open by appointment. Constance and Bob Wood. Small furniture, Americana, Indian artifacts, metalware, copper and brass, Oriental including netsuke and woodblock prints; baseball memorabilia (not cards). Prices range from $25 to $2,500; most are $100 to $300.

In Peterborough:

Brennans Antiques, 130 Hunt Road, Peterborough, NH 03458. Tel: (603) 924-3445. Open by appointment. Joseph and Judith Brennan. Primitives, tin, woodenware, tools, furniture, quilts, and so on. Prices from $1 to $500.

The Cobbs Antiques, 83 Grove Street, Peterborough, NH 03458. Tel: (603) 924-6361. Open 9:30-5 Mo-Fr. Charles and Dudley Cobb. In business for over fifteen years. Offers 18th and 19th century American country and formal furniture and accessories. Prices start at $10.

Old Town Farm Antiques, 121B Old Town Farm Road, Peterborough, NH 03458. Tel: (603) 924-3523. Open daily 10-5. Robert S. Taylor, Hope Taylor. This fifteen-year-old shop features primitives, Early American antiques, Oriental rugs. 4,500 sq. ft.

The Pastime Porch of The Game Preserve, 110 Spring Road, Peterborough, NH 03458. Tel: (603) 924-6710. Open by chance or by appointment. Lee and Rally Dennis. Games, childhood memorabilia, books, tin, wood, Americana. Prices from $5 to $150.

In West Swanzey:

Knotty Pine Antique Market, Rte. 10, West Swanzey, NH 03469. Tel: (603) 352-5252. Open 9-5 daily. Joan E. Pappas. Knotty Pine is 200 shops of antiques and collectibles under one roof. Prices range from $1 to thousands.

Manchester & Environs

Manchester is New Hampshire's largest city (pop. 85,119) and its most important manufacturing center. The largest textile mill in the world was built alongside the Merrimack River during the 19th century and was the city's major employer until it closed permanently in 1935. A group of local investors bought the mile-long stretch of red brick buildings and today it is home to dozens of smaller industries.

What to See

·*The Currier Gallery of Art*, 192 Orange Street. One of the finest museums in all New England, the Currier is a Renaissance-style limestone and marble building which houses fine collections of American decorative arts and paintings, as well as European paintings. The first floor features the American collection which includes excellent examples of 18th and 19th century New Hampshire furniture, silver by the Reveres, Samuel Edwards, and Jacob Hurd, Early American glassware and pewter, and paintings by Stuart, Bierstadt, Wyeth, and Hopper. On the second floor is an excellent collection of Flemish and Italian master paintings and drawings, including drawings by Tiepolo, Pietro Perugino's *Madonna and Child*, and a truly superb scupture called *Seated Nude* by Henri Matisse. Open 10-4 (10-10 on Th); 2-5 on Su. Closed Mo. No admission charge.

Manchester Historic Association, 129 Amherst Street. This local history museum has a collection of more than 3,500 rare and unusual books, and good collections of toys, guns, and old fire-fighting equipment. Open Tu-Fr 11-4; Sa 10-4. Free.

Amoskeag Mills. During the late 19th century, this massive textile complex turned out a mile of cotton cloth a minute in its heyday. Constructed between 1838 and 1915 by the Amoskeag Manufacturing Company, the mile-long complex of forty brick buildings was the world's largest until the Depression put it under. It was one of the first American companies to provide its workers with decent housing, although wages and conditions might seem exploitative by today's standards. May of the worker tenements have been privately purchased and renovated into attractive apartments. The Manchester Historic Association conducts tours of the millyards. Contact the association for details.

Zimmerman House, 223 Heather Street. One of the few examples of Frank Lloyd Wright's "Prairie Style" architecture to be found in the Northeast, this 1951 home exhibits floating concrete slab design and other characteristics unique to the master builder.

Where to Shop

In Bedford:

Bell Hill Antiques, Rte. 101, Bedford, NH 03102. Tel: (603) 472-5580. Open daily 10-5:30. Doris Marks, Manager. Bell Hill is a group of twenty dealers specializing in country furniture and decorative accessories along with some formal items and chinoiserie. Prices range from $5 to $3,000.

In Manchester:

End of the Trail Antiques, 420 Chestnut Street, Manchester, NH 03101. Tel: (603) 669-1238. Open Mo-Sa 10-4:30; closed Su. June and Fred Kos. This twenty-year-old shop offers a general line, specializing in furniture.

Portsmouth & Environs _____

Located at the mouth of the Piscataqua River, Portsmouth is New Hampshire's only seaport and its most historic town. The city was established as a township in 1631 and before the Revolution served as the seat of British provincial government. Blessed with access to the sea and an abundance of timber from the north, the town rose to prominence as a shipbuilding and commercial center during the 19th century. The vintage mansions that line Middle Street are reminders of the great days of the West Indian trade. This is one of the best places in New England to see great old architectural gems restored to their former glory.

What to See

MacPheadris-Warner House, 150 Daniel Street. Built in 1716 by the Scottish sea captain and merchant Archibald MacPheadris, this gorgeous Georgian mansion is the oldest brick house in the city and possibly the most magnificent brick town house in America. Its central hallways are decorated with murals by an unknown hand, including a life-size protrait of two Mohawk chiefs who went to London with Peter Schuyler in 1710 to be presented to Queen Anne. Fine European and New England-made furnishings are on hand, and there are splendid portraits of the Warner family by painter Joseph Blackburn. Behind the house is St. John's Church and a cemetery known as God's Little Acre. Guided tours 10-5 Mo-Sa; 10-2 Su from mid-May to mid October. Admission is $1.50.

The Moffatt-Ladd House, 154 Market Street. Captain John Moffatt had this Georgian mansion--modeled after his old homestead in Hertfordshire, England--built as a wedding gift for his son in 1764. Alas, the son skipped to the West Indies to avoid paying some debts a few years later leaving behind his bride who lived there with Captain and Mrs. Moffatt until joining her wayward husband. William Whipple, a signer of the Declaration of Independence, lived here from 1768 to 1785. The house's grand entrance, its rich ornamented stair hall, and original "Bay of Naples" wallpaper printed in Paris in 1815, testify to the comfortable lifestyle of the mercantile class of early Portsmouth. Out back is one of the oldest English gardens still in its original forms. The house is owned by the Society of Colonial Dames of New Hampshire. Guided tours Mo-Sa 10-4; Su 2-5 from June 15 to October 15. Admission is $2.

The Wentworth-Gardner House, 140 Mechanic Street. Built for the younger borther of the state's last royal governor in 1760, this Georgian mansion is notable for its intricate carvings, paneling, balusters, and cornices--a testimony to the high art of the ship's carpenters who constructed it. Hand-painted paper in the dining room and four restored rooms, complete with fireplaces, are evidence of the elegance of another era. The rich interior woodwork, including wide clapborad floors rusticated to imitate cut stone, are believed to have taken eighteen months to complete. Guided tour Tu-Sa 10-5; 12-5 Su. Admission is $1.50.

Governor John Langdon House, 143 Pleasant Street. George Washington slept here in 1789 and remarked that his host had the "handsomest house in Portsmouth." Langdon was a prosperous local merchant who served as first president of the United States Senate. Built in 1784, this handsome Georgian mansion--surrounded by impeccably landscaped grounds--is crowned by a striking Chinese Chippendale balustrade. Its interior is distinguished by intricate carvings and furnished with antiques. Open June 1 to October 15 daily. Guided tours from 10-5. Admission is $1.50.

John Paul Jones House, 43 Middle Street. Now the headquarters of the Portsmouth Historical Society, this two-story frame house was built in 1758 by Captain Purcell whose widow kept it as a boarding house after his death. Among her tenants was John Paul Jones who stayed here while overseeing construction of the *Ranger* on Badger's Island in 1777. Guided tours are conducted by hostesses in colonial garb who'll show you fine early furnishings, china, and historical memorabilia, in addition to the room where Jones stayed. Open June 1 to October 15 Mo-Sa 10-5. Admission is $1.50.

Richard Jackson House, Northwest Street. Built in 1664,

this medieval-looking saltbox with its weathered clapboards is the oldest home in the city. Its interior is sparse with exposed beam ceilings and wide floor boards. Open only by appointment. Call (603) 227-3956.

Portsmouth Athenaeum, 9 Market Street. One of the nation's best preserved public buildings, this 1805 Federal is distinguished by the traditional four tall chimneys and widow's walk. In addition to its 30,000 volume library of rare and historical books, this museum has a fine collection of ship models, including the *Clovis* carved from whalebone, and a 1749 model of H.M.S. *America.* Open Th 1-4; Tu by appointment. Tel: (603) 431-2538. Free.

Strawbery Banke. When the first group of English settlers arrived here in 1623, the riverbanks were covered with wild strawberries. They decided to call their community "Strawbery Banke" and it was not until several decades later that the name was changed to Portsmouth. A ten-acre urban renewal project covering the Puddle Dock area--site of the original settlement--Strawbery Banke is an often cited example of the triumph of preservation over demolition. The whole area was slated for destruction in the late 1950s until a group of determined citizens waged a long, and successful, battle to restore the district instead. Several houses have been completely restored, others are still in the process of renovation. The emphasis in the district is on "living history" and several craftsmen now ply their trades here. Among the things to see:

Captain John Shelburne House. Built around 1695, this attractive dwelling is the oldest house on the Banke. It fea-

tures a detailed exhibit on the construction and restoration of the house.

Stephen Chase House. A beautiful Georgian built by a wealthy merchant around 1762, this mansion is notable for its handsomely carved frontispiece and interior wood carvings, believed to be the handiwork of William Deering, a ship carver from nearby Kittery, ME.

Captain Keyran Walsh House. A Federal "double house"--two chimneys and a central hall--this 1796 sea captain's home is noted for its beautiful staircase and splendid painting and marbling of the interior woodwork. It's modestly furnished with Federal and Chippendale furniture.

Governor Goodwin Mansion. Constructed in 1811 and one of the few houses moved to Strawbery Banke, this is the area's most elegant structure. The mansion is furnished as it would have been when the Goodwins lived in it from 1832-82. It contains Victorian furniture, family portraits, family heirlooms, and a miniature figurine exhibit.

Strawbery Banke is open 9:30-5 daily between April 15 and November 15. Admission is $4.50 for adults; $1.50 for children under fifteen.

Where to Shop

In Newington:

J. and J. Hanrahan, ABBA, Old Dover Road, Newington, NH 03801. Tel: (603) 436-6234. Jack Hanrahan. This twenty-three-year old shop specializes in used and rare books, prints, paintings. Prices range from $4 to $3,500.

In Portsmouth:

M.S. Carter, Inc., 175 Market Street, Portsmouth, NH 03801. Tel: (603) 436-1781. Open 10-5 Mo-Sa. Margaret S. Carter. In business for over twenty-five years, Carter features country furniture and accessories, decoys, old toys. Near Strawbery Banke. Prices from $5 to $5,000.

Tidewater Antiques, 117 Market Street, Portsmouth, NH 03801. Tel: (603) 431-5030. Open 10-4 except Su. Helen C. Jarvis. General antiques and collectibles; tools a specialty. Prices run from $10 to $1,000.

Rhode Island

Providence •

Bristol

N. Kingston •

W. Kingston •

Newport

Block Island

Rhode Islanders are fond of pointing out that America's War of Independence really had its roots in their state. A year before the Boston Tea Party--on June 9, 1772--a band of Providence citizens reacted to English legislation to limit American shipping by forcing the British revenue schooner *Gaspee* aground at Warwick, burning the vessel, the capturing its crew. Rhode Island citizens declared their independence on May 4, 1776--two months before the rest of the colonies.

No state in New England offers collectors more to see in a more compact space. The College Hill Historic District in Providence, for example, is the largest gathering of intact Early American homes in the nation. The great mansions of Newport, built by America's wealthiest families in the years following the Civil War as summer "cottages," are completely unique. Such conspicuous evidence of the power of pre-income tax wealth simply cannot be found in such abundance anywhere else in the United States. Brown University has collections of Early American books and manuscripts that are the finest in existence. In short, Rhode Island is a giant delight for collectors and American history buffs.

Block Island

After you've exhausted yourself with the mansions of Newport and the College Hill Historic District in Providence, you may need a place to relax for a few days. This beautiful and wild island, located twelve miles south of the mainland and occupied by fewer than 500 souls, is just the place. Named for a Dutch explorer named Adrian Block who sailed these parts in 1614, the island was first settled toward the end of the 17th century. After a brief vogue as a coastal resort in the late 19th century, Block Island has retreated to its sleepy glory. Great beaches, deep water fishing, and a few historic structures are its charm.

What to See

Old Harbor Historic District. Most of the town of New Shoreham is included in this district which once housed many famous old Victorian hotels; also, most of them since ravaged by fire. See *The Spring House*, one of the excellent examples of Victoriana still standing on the island. Built in 1852 and greatly expanded in the 1870s, this three-story resort hotel has a flared mansard roof, cupola, and great full-length veranda. For furnishings, see the *Hotel Manisses* on Spring Street (see Where to Stay), just renovated to its former elegance. The pretty *Surf Cottage* on Dodge Street was built in 1876. It has an elaborate mansard roof and three large Gothic dormers. Nearby is *Woonsocket House*, an 1870s boarding house which now headquarters the Block Island Historical Society.

Mohegan Bluffs. The south shore of Block Island is shaped by a series of spectacular multicolored cliffs with steep paths leading down to the sea.

Block Island North Light. Located at Sandy Point, now a bird and wildlife preserve covering twenty-eight acres, this 1867 lighthouse was built of Connecticut granite hauled to the site by oxen. With its eighteen inch thick walls, this lighthouse has manged to resist the ravages of the sea--something three predecessors on the same spot were not able to do. Abandoned since 1970, locals are now attempting to renovate the site and turn it into a maritime museum.

Where to Stay

The Hotel Manisses, Spring Street, Block Island, RI 02807. Tel: (401) 466-2421 or 466-2836. Seventeen rooms with private baths; four with jacuzzis. Prices run $60 to $100 with double, queen or king-sized beds; $135 to $150 with jacuzzi. Reservations as far in advance as possible. Owners: Joan and Justin Abrams. Rates include full buffet breakfast and wine and nibbles hour.

Built in 1874, this is one of the truly fine examples of a great Victorian resort hotel. Furnished with authentic period furniture, the lobby is distinguished by large arches. Generous amounts of stained glass are scattered throughout. Lovingly restored by Joan and Justin Abrams, their daughter Rita Draper and her husband Steve over a period of five years, the Manisses looks as good as it must have in its turn-of-the-century salad days. The Abrams family also own *The 1661 Inn*, a twenty-five-room hotel just across the street, which they've been operating for fifteen years. It has Colonial decor and many rooms have private decks overlooking the Atlantic. Meals for both hotels are served at the Manisses. Rates at The 1661 Inn run $45 to $80 for a shared bath; $75 to $135 for a private bath and include a full buffet breakfast and wine and nibbles hour. A great place to visit in any season of the year.

Newport & Environs

The very name of America's most famous summer resort has come to symbolize an aura of luxury and opulence. True, the very rich who once occupied the great mansions that line Bellevue and Ocean avenues are long gone. But it is still easier to find someone to repair a Mercedes than to fix a pair of Guccis. Before the Civil War, Newport was the place where southern planters and their ladies took respite from the hot summer sun. After the War, the Vanderbilts and Astors and Belmonts showed up, their heads filled with visions of the palaces and chateaux they had seen in Europe while on the "grand tour." They commissioned the nation's best architects to build "cottages" of incredible magnificence. The "400" was born here because Mrs. William Astor's ballroom held no more than 400 people and, obviously, anyone who couldn't squeeze in simply didn't count. This is the best place in the world to see how the other 1 percent lived.

What to See

The Breakers, Ochre Point Avenue. The grandest of them all, this seventy-room palace was designed for Cornelius Vanderbilt II, grandson of the Commodore who made his fortune in railroads and steamships, by architect Richard Morris Hunt. Begun in 1895, the place is a mosaic of French and Italian marble, ornate fireplaces, antique tapestries, silver and gold gilded ceilings, immense Oriental rugs, crystal chandeliers. If it cost a lot, Hunt used it in the house. The "Great Hall" soars two stories up to a ceiling painted to represent the sky. The *Grand Salon*, or music room, was built and decorated in France, taken apart and shipped to Newport, and then reassembled in The Breakers. The two-story high *Dining Room*, with its warm red alabaster, bronze and gilt glow, and ceiling painted to represent Aurora at Dawn, has a table that could seat a modest thirty-four people for a light snack. It's almost enough to make you believe in income tax. Open April to October 10-5 daily; We and Su, until 8 July to mid-September. Guided tours are $3.50.

Marble House, Bellevue Avenue. Another Richard Morris Hunt design, this white marble "cottage" was built by William K. Vanderbilt--Cornelius' brother--for his wife Alva at a cost of two million 19th century dollars for the house and another nine million for the furnishings. When they divorced a few years after the house was completed in 1892, she got to keep it. It was here that the former Mrs. Vanderbilt, the Mrs. O.H.P. Belmont, threw Newport's most memorable party--a ten course soiree for her friends and their pets, all seated at the same table. The menu included stewed liver and rice, and shredded dog biscuits. All of which proves that Scott Fitzgerald was right: the rich really are different from you and me. The most ornate of Hunt's designs, Marble House is thought to have been modeled after the Petit Trianon at Versailles, or perhaps after the White House. Its *Gold Ballroom*, swathed in gold gilt panels with glittering crystal chandeliers and mirrors, is the most ornate in all of Newport. Then you'll want to see the *Harold S. Vanderbilt Memorial Room* with its yachting trophies and memorabilia and the *Gothic Room*, where the family's collection of medieval art is displayed. And, of course, there's the *Dining Room*--scene of Mrs. Belmont's howling success. Each of the solid bronze Louis XIV chairs weighs sixty pounds so it was necessary to provide each guest with a servant to move the chair when he or she wanted to leave the table.

Belcourt Castle, Bellevue Avenue. Before Oliver Hazard Perry Belmont married Alva Smith Vanderbilt, who had tossed her husband out of Marble House in Newport's most sensational divorce, he was hardly wanting for a place to live. The ubiquetous Richard Morris Hunt based his plans for this immense estate on a Louis XIII hunting lodge he had seen in France. Completed in 1891, each of the castle's rooms is decorated in a different period of Italian, French, or English design. The "Grand Stair" is a handcarved authentic reproduction of one found in the Musee de Cluny in Paris. For collectors, this may be the most interesting of all the Newport houses because of its outstanding gathering of European furnishings, the largest private collection of stained glass in America, and a striking collection of medieval armor. The Royal Arts Foundation displays its splendid collection of French furniture and silver here--the most impressive single object being a 23-karat gold Royal Coronation Coach, decorated with oil paintings, and weighing four tons. Open July to Labor Day 9-6; April through June and September through November 10-5; closed December through March. Guided tours are $3.

The Elms, Bellevue Avenue. Coal baron E.J. Berwind was the son of poor German immigrants and an outsider to Newport society who regarded him as "nouveau riche." This stately chateau, modeled after the Chateau d'Asnieres near Paris, was his bid for respectability. Built by architect Horace Trumbauer, the housewarming given by the Berwinds in 1901 was the highlight of the season. After his death, his sister Julia Berwind used the house and became one of the last grand dames of Newport society. The house was slated for the wrecker's ball in 1962 but was saved by the Preservation Society of Newport County which raised enough money to buy the house and replace its original furnishings which had been auctioned off for $486,000. You'll want to see the 18th century tapestries woven at the Imperial Russian Tapestry Manufactured in Leningrad which are hanging in an upstairs hallway. Open daily 10-5 from May to October; Sa until 8 from July to mid-September. Guided tours are $3.

Chateau-sur-Mer, Bellevue Avenue. Built in 1852 for China Trade merchant William S. Wetmore, this lavish mansion is widely considered one of the finest Victorian homes in America. The original structure, designed by Seth Bradford, was enlarged in 1872 by, who else, Richard Morris Hunt. The home was in the Wetmore family until the early 1960s and many of the furnishing are original, including a splendid collection of Rose Mandarin and Rose Medallion china sets and a collection of Victorian toys and dollhouses. Open daily 10-5 from May to October; Fri until 8 from July to mid-September. Admission is $3.

Kingscote, Bellevue Avenue and Bowery Street. Designed in 1839 by Richard Upjohn, this irregular frame mansion was commissioned by a southern planter George Noble Jones, then sold in the 1860s to William H. King. It is considered the nation's first summer "cottage" in what was to become the American Royalty manner. Its best feature is a dining room that King had McKim, Mead, and White add in 1881, complete with a Tiffany glass wall and cork ceiling. The house also contains a splendid collection of Oriental paintings, rugs, porcelain, and Townsend-Goddard furniture. Open daily 10-5 from May to October; Admission is $3 until 8.

Rosecliff, Bellevue Avenue. In 1891 Mrs. Herman Oelrichs, daughter of Jim Fair, one of the discoverers of the Comstock Lode, moved to Newport with her husband and bought the Rosecliff estate. Tessie Oelrichs--whose sister Birdie later married William K. Vanderbilt--found the house a bit too modest and commissioned Stanford White to do something a bit more elaborate. The result is perhaps the most tasteful of all the Newport mansions, a dazzling imitation of the Grand Trianon at Versailles. Designed primarily for entertaining, the house's eighty-by-forty-foot ballroom is the largest in Newport. Open daily 10-5 from April to October; Mo until 8 from July to mid-September. Admission is $3.

Hammersmith Farm, Ocean Drive. Hardly the fanciest of Newport mansions, this twenty-eight-room shingle-style cottage built in 1887 was formerly owned by Mrs. Hugh Auchincloss, mother of Jacqueline Kennedy. President and Mrs. Kennedy were married in Newport and celebrated their marriage here at the farm--so called because the fifty rolling acres surrounding the house have been farmed since 1640. The gardens were designed by Frederick Olmsted. The house contains many momentoes from the years that Jacqueline lived here as a child and later with her husband and children. Guided tours 10-5 April to October; until 8 from Memorial Day to Labor Day. Admission is $3.

Colonial Newport. Once you've completed the grand tour of Newport mansions, you've still got a full day's work ahead of you. Downtown Newport is one of the nation's greatest treasuries of Colonial structures, many of them the handiwork of mast carpenter Richard Munday or famed Colonial architect Peter Harrison, whose credits also include Boston's King's Chapel and Christ Church in Cambridge. Start with Harrison's *Brick Market* at Long Wharf and Thames Street. Built between 1762 and 1772, this handsome building was the commercial center of Newport. The main floor was used as a market and watchhouse, the upper floors were reserved for offices and storage. Nearby on Washington Square is the *Old Colony House*, designed by Richard Munday, in 1739. It was here that the Rhode Island legislature declared itself independent of George III on May 4, 1776, making Rhode Island the first colony to do so. You'll find some fine examples of Townsend-Goddard furniture inside and one of Gilbert Stuart's full-length portraits of Geoge Washington. Proof of Rhode Island's religious tolerance is the *Touro Synagogue*, 85 Touro Street, built by Peter Harrison in 1763, and the first Jewish synagogue in the New World. Nearby, and often overlooked, is the *Wanton-Lyman-Hazard House* at 17 Broadway, built around 1695 and the oldest restored home in Newport. *Trinity Church*, which rises above Queen Anne Square, was designed by Richard Munday who modeled it after Old North Church in Boston, itself a steal from Christopher Wren. Built in 1725-26 , it is probably the best example of Colonial religious architecture in the nation. You'll want to see the *International Tennis Hall of Fame*, 194 Bellevue Avenue, for its collection of tennis memorabilia. Once called the Newport Casino and designed by Stanford White in 1880, this shingle-style commercial structure was the site of the original U.S. Open and its twelve handsome grass courts are the only ones in the country open to the general public. Adjacent is the *Newport Automobile Museum*, which features the largest collection of antique autombles in New England. The most mysterious building in America is the *Old Stone Mill* in Touro Park. Speculation about its origins range from Vikings to Indians to Portuguese and its age from three hundred to eight hundred years old. The most recent theory is that it was built by Governor Benedict Arnold as a windmill around 1673. Nobody really knows.

Other Sights. If you still have energy left after Newport, you may want to explore some of the nearby town. The Colonial town of Bristol has a splendid *Waterfront Historic District*, including more than four hundred historic buildings. See especially *Linden Place*, 500 Hope Street, designed by famed architect Russell Warren for General George DeWolf. This magnificent Federal structure was completed in 1810. The *Bristol County Jail*, 48 Court Street, houses the library and collections of the Bristol Historical and Preservation Society, including costumes, Revolutionary war relics, portraits, costumes, and a children's museum. If you can bear one more mansion, try *Blitheworld Gardens and Arboretum*, on Ferry Road, the Victorian summer estate of Majorie Van Wickle Lyon. Not as fancy as its Newport counterparts, the estate is distinguished, nonetheless, by thirty-three beautifully landscaped acres of grounds that extend down to Bristol Harbor and overlook Narragansett Bay. The grounds are open from January to December 10-4 Tu-Su. Admission is $1.50. A

bit further afield, but worth a visit, is the *Wickford Historic District* in North Kingstown. Established in the 1840s as a trading post by Richard Smith, an associate of Roger Williams, Wickford has a fine sampling of 18th and 19th century buildings. See, especially, the *Old Narragansett Church*, 60 Church Lane, built in 1707.

Where to Stay

The Inn at Castle Hill, Ocean Drive, Newport, RI 02840. Tel: (401) 849-3800. Ten rooms in winter; twenty in summer, seventeen with baths. Rates range from $40 to $195 depending on season. Reservations should be made several months in advance. Onwer: T. Paul McEnroe.

For a taste of what it must have been like to live in a Newport mansion, this is a good place to start. Built as a private home for the renowned naturalist Alexander Agassiz in 1874, this magnificent estate located on a penisula where the Atlantic funnels into Narragansett Bay was a forerunner of the grander homes to come. Many of the building's original furnishings remain and the Oriental rugs and handcrafted wood paneling serve as striking reminders of a bygone Victorian era. A wonderful fireplace of inlaid woodwork dominates the sitting room with its handsome oak bar. Paul McEnroe has deliberately kept the number of guest rooms to a minimum to enhance the sense of spaciousness of the home. Bedrooms are oversized and airy, with breathtaking views of Newport Harbor and the Atlantic, and many of the baths are as large as a normal hotel room. The Inn's dining room is open for dinner Th-Sa in April and May; Mo-Sa June through October; for lunch Tu-Sa from Memorial Day to November 1; for Sunday brunch April through November. Featuring continental cuisine, this is one of the best places in Newport to eat but be sure to make reservations. Gentlemen need ties and jeans are a no-no. Located close to everything, this is one of the best.

Where to Shop

In Bristol:
Alfred's, 331 Hope Street, Bristol, RI 02809. Tel: (401) 253-3465. Open daily 10-5. Alfred Brazil. This fifteen-year-old

shop offers flow blue, art glass, lamps, pattern glass, silver, and furniture. Prices are $5 to $2,000.

In Newport:

A and A Gaines, 40 Franklin Street, Newport, RI 02840. Tel: (401) 849-6844, 846-0538. Open 11-5 Tu-Sa. Alan and Amy Gaines. In businesss for twenty-eight years, the Gaines feature period furniture, clocks, nautical items, China trade items. Prices range from $100 to $10,000, with emphasis on items priced at $300 to $5,000.

Alice Simpson Antiques, 40½ Franklin Street, Newport, RI 02840. Tel: (401) 849-4252. Open 11-5 Mo-Sa. Alice Simpson. Victorian Silverplate, textiles, furniture. Prices run from $5 to $500.

Anchor and Dolphin Books, 20 Franklin Street, PO Box 823, Newport, RI 02840. Tel: (401) 846-6890. Open most afternoons and by appointment. James A. Hinck, Ann Marie Wall. Specialist in rare books. Prices range from $1 to several thousand.

The Antique Center, 42 Spring Street, Newport, RI 02840. Tel: (401) 847-3968. Open daily 10:30-5. Mary B. Fay. In business for twenty-two years. Stereo cards, R.S. Prussia, Staffordshire, cut glass, pressed glass, silver, clocks, lamps, daguerreotypes, Royal Doulton, furniture, Royal Worcester, Dresden, Canton, etc. Prices from 50¢ to $850.

Aunt Annie's, 71 Touro Street, Newport, RI 02840. Tel: (401) 849-2808. Open 10-2 Mo-We and 1-4 Fr and Sa; closed Su. Ann T. Cunningham. This shop offers dollhouses, miniatures. Prices start at $2.

E's Emporium, 62 Spring Street, Newport, RI 02840. Tel: (401) 846-3361. Open 10-5; Su 12-5. Elizabeth A. Horton. Depression glass, country kitchen collectibles, linen. Prices run from $1 to $50.

Etc. Etc., 65 Touro Street, Newport, RI 02840. Tel: (401) 846-9024. Open 11-5 except We and Su. Florence Archambault. Etc. Etc. sells original graphics, depression glass, occupied Japan, antiques. Prices range from $1 to $450.

Gallery '76 Antiques, Inc., 83 Spring Street, Newport, RI 02840. Tel: (401) 847-4288. Open 10-5:30 except Su. Barbara Leis. This shop features late 18th and early 19th century American furniture, Oriental export, English porcelains and lamps, silver, jewelry. Prices from $10 to $5,000.

Harvinidge, 74 Spring Street, Newport, RI 02840. Tel: (401) 849-2076. Open by appointment only. Marjorie L. Smith. Specializes in British commemoratives (royal). Prices range from $10 to $800.

John Larner Antiques, 44 Franklin Street, Newport, RI 02840. Tel: (401) 849-2680. Open 11-5 Tu-Sa. John Larner. General line. Prices start at $100.

Lamplighter Antiques, 42 Spring Street, Newport, RI 02840. Tel: (401) 849-4179. Open 12-5 Mo-Sa. Al Lozito. This shop offers oil lamps, clocks, prints, furniture, and accessories. Prices from $5 to $2,000.

Newport Exchange, 626 Thames Street, Newport, RI 02840. Tel: (401) 847-0966. Open 10-6 Mo-Sa. Lillian R. Gee and Laurice S. Parfet. Prices range from 50¢ to $500.

The Nostalgia Factory, Brick Market Place, Newport, RI 02840. Tel: (401) 849-3441. Open 10-6 daily October to May; 10-10 June to September. Rudy Franchi. This fifteen-year-old shop sells original old advertising, posters, signs, political buttons, royalty items, ephemera. Prices from $1 to $850.

Ruskin Antiques, 33 Franklin Street, Newport, RI 02840. Tel: (401) 847-6620. Arthur Ruskin formerly 140 Charles St., Boston, MA. In business for over thirty years. Period furniture and decorative accessories, English, European, Oriental.

In North Kingston:

Potpourri, 20 Main Street, Wickford, North Kingston, RI 02852. Tel: (401) 295-0891. Open 10-5 Mo-Sa; Su 12-5. Paul C. Carlson. General line of antiques, gifts, and reproductions.

In West Kingston

J.P. Greene Fine Woodworks, PO Box 286, James Trail, West Kingston, RI 02892. Tel: (401) 783-6614. Open by appointment. Jeffrey P. Greene. Handcrafted furniture of 18th century design. Prices run from $49 to $3,800.

Peter Pots Pottery and Peter Pots Authentic Americana, 101 Glen Rock Road, West Kingston, RI 02892. Tel: (401) 783-2350. Open Mo-Sa 10-4; Su 1-4. O.W. Greene, III. In buisness for thirty-six years, this shop features its own handcrafted stoneware, country primitives. Prices range from $2 to $2,000; average under $100.

Providence

Rhode Island's first settlement--and future capital--was founded in 1636 by Roger Williams, a young English minister whose views that "no man should be molested for his conscience" had given offense to the good Puritans in the nearby Massachusetts Bay Colony. By 1643, settlements based on Williams' tenets of freedom of conscience had been started in Newport, Warwick, and Portsmouth as well. Originally a farming community, Providence had developed into a major shipping and commercial port by the mid-18th century. Today, Providence (pop. 160,982) is the second largest city in New England and a center of industry and business.

What to See

College Hill Historic District. In an effort to relieve the congestion that developed along the early city's waterfront, the city fathers of the early 18th century decided to widen a dirt path that ran up a steep hill behind the commercial district. *Benefit Street*, this, became the key to opening up what is now called *College Hill*, a predominantly residential neighborhood containing what is widely believed to be the largest collection of intact early buildings in the nation. Along these tree-shaded streets, you'll find every architectural style from Colonial to Italianate to Greek Revival. Among the many treasures to see is the *John Brown House*, 52 Power Street. The Brown family--four brothers--were to become the most influential settlers in Providence. John, who lived in this spectacular mansion designed and built in 1786 by his architect brother Joseph, was a wealthy merchant and the first man to open up the China Trade from this port. Another brother, Moses, a Quaker, established the Providence Bank and was the first financier of the textile industry in the United States. Nicholas, the fourth Brown brother, founded Rhode Island College, today known as Brown University, in 1764. Restored by the Rhode Island Historical Society, this spacious three-story Georgian mansion contains a splendid collection of Rhode Island furnishings, many of them Brown family pieces. Most spectacular is a nine-shell blockfront secretary by John

Goddard, one of the finest pieces of Colonial furniture to be found anywhere.

First Baptist Church, 75 North Main Street. Joseph Brown cribbed his design for this two-story clapboard Georgian from an unexecuted plan for St. Martin's-in-the-Fields in London. Roger Williams built the first Baptist church in the nation on this site in 1700. It was replaced by this structure in 1774-75. Guided tours 10-3 Su-Fr from April to October; 10-noon on Sa.

Brick School House, 24 Meeting Street. Erected in 1769, this two-story brick and frame Georgian was the first, temporary home of Brown University and later became one of the first free schools in the nation. Today, it is the headquarters of the Providence Preservaton Society.

Brown University, College and Prospect Street. The seventh-oldest college in the United States, Brown was founded as Rhode Island College in 1764 and renamed for its major benefactor Nicholas Brown in 1804. It was the first college in the nation to advocate complete religious freedom. A collector's delight, the campus is home to many superb buildings and collections. Among them: the *John Carter Brown Library*, which houses an outstanding collection of Early American history. Its collection of Americana printed during the Colonial period is probably the nation's finest. The *John Hay Library* has what is probably the best collection of Abraham Lincoln's books and manuscripts, as well as a virtually complete collection of the writing of John Hay, Lincoln's secretary. The *Annmary Brown Memorial* features Brown family heirlooms and letters. The *John D. Rockefeller, Jr. Library* has an outstanding Chinese collection. All told, Brown's libraries well over two million books.

Rhode Island School of Design, 2 College Street. Founded in 1877, obstensibly to train artisans for industry, the RISD is today one of the most prestigious art schools in the U.S. The college has a superb *Museum of Art* noted for its fine collections of classical art, 19th century American and French paintigs, Oriental costumes, and European decorative arts. There's also a fine collection of 20th century art on the lower level with works by Picasso, Matisse, and other reknowned artists. Adjoining the museum--in its own building, a 1904 replica of a Georgian mansion--is the outstanding *Charles Pendleton* collection of 18th century American furnishing and decorative arts. Pendleton was a successful Providence lawyer who had a life-long love affair with antiques. He donated his collection to the school in 1904 with the stipulation that they be housed in a new building constructed as nearly as possible to duplicate his residence. One room on the ground floor is devoted exclusively to the arts of Rhode Island and features the work of the most famous Colonial cabinetmakers Job Townsend and John Goddard. The museum and Pendleton House are located at 224 Benefit Street. Open September 1 to June 15 Tu-We-Fr-Sa 10:30-5; Th 1-9; Su 2-5. The rest of the year We-Sa only 11-4. Admission is $1, Sa free.

Where to Shop

Pre-Amble, 736 Hope Street, Providence, RI 02906. Tel: (401) 274-1322. Open 10-5:30 Mo-Sa. Alfred Luchesi, Jr. Near Brown University and the Rhode Island School of Design Museum, this twenty-year-old shop features furniture and accessories. Prices range from $5 to $5,000.

Vermont

- Burlington
- Stowe
- Shelburne
- Montpelier
- E. Montpelier
- Barre
- E. Barre
- Middlebury
- Brandon
- Woodstock
- Danby
- Grafton
- Manchester
- Newfane
- Bennington
- Brattleboro

When the French explorer Samuel de Champlain first saw the lush forests extending southward from the lake that now bears his name, he is said to have exclaimed "les verts monts." That was in 1609 but the name stuck. More than a century later "les verts monts"--the green mountains--was anglicized to Vermont and became the official name of the region.

Vermont's most famous literary figure is probably the poet Robert Frost who spent his summers on a farm near Ripton and wrote many of his best works about country life there. Frost is buried in the graveyard of the First Congregational Church in Bennington.

Vermont is a place where village life still dominates. It has no major industrial centers and the largest city--Burlington--has a population of only 40,000. Its backroads, rolling green farmland, and covered bridges are picture-postcard descriptions of early New England life.

The state's best destination for the collector is the extraordinary treasure chest of Early American life known as the Shelburne Museum, located just south of Burlington nears the shores of Lake Champlain. It just may be the best collection of pure Americana to be found anywhere.

Bennington, Brattleboro, & Newfane ___

The small, friendly cities of Bennington and Brattleboro serve mainly as urban rest stops for travelers touring the charming villages of southern Vermont but both possess considerable charm of their own and should not be overlooked.

Brattleboro was the first permanent settlement in Vermont (1724) and has a fine museum and art center. Bennington is probably best-known to collectors as the city where Grandma Moses went to school as a young girl and where one of the best collections of her work is now on display. Newfane is a pretty little village deep in the nearby Green Mountains and the site of one of New England's most charming inns.

What to See

Brattleboro Museum and Art Center, Old Railroad Station. Housed in a renovated railroad station, this city museum features historical and art exhibits. On display are examples of the Estey organ, manufactured in Brattleboro from 1853 until the company closed down in 1961, in what had been the world's largest organ factory. Open May to mid-December Tu-Su 12-4.

Old Bennington Country Store. A Bennington tradition since 1793, this charming shop has been located several places over the years but still offers old-fashioned New England general store goods, including penny candy, old-style wooden toys, cast-iron cookware, and fancy cheeses.

Bennington Museum, West Main Street. One of New England's finest regional museums, this is a diverse collection that includes choice examples of fine American glassware, 19th century pottery and porcelain, and the oldest American flag in existence--the Bennington Flag--which flew above the Continental Storehouse during the Battle of Bennington in 1775. The museum's furniture collection includes a rare Hadley hope chest (one of only 115 known to exist) made in the 17th century. And, of course, there is the museum's outstanding collection of more than thirty Grandma Moses paintings. Adjacent to the museum is a recreation of the schoolhouse the artist--born Anna Mary Robertson Moses--once attended. Open March to November 9-5; closed major holidays. Admission is $2.

Where to Stay

The Four Columns Inn, 230 West Street, Newfane, VT 05345. Tel: (802) 365-7713. Nine rooms with bath, two suites with bath, one cottage (two bedrooms, living room, and bath). Rates: $50 to $85 a night, including continental breakfast. Reservations should be made several months in advance; one year for fall leaf season. Owners: Sandra and Jacques Allembert.

Originally built in 1830 by General Pardon Kimball for his Southern wife, supposedly a replica of her girlhood home, the house, known for many years as *Kimball Hall*, was built of virgin timbers without plans. The main house and barn were renovated and opened as an inn and restaurant in 1965. All decor is traditional Colonial, mixed with many fine French and American antiques, and there are many old brass beds, four-posters, and canopy beds. The inn's restaurant specializes in French cuisine with a nouvelle touch and is one of the most highly-regarded in New England. This is the best place in the universe to watch nature's fall changing of colors. Located twelve miles north of Brattleboro.

Where to Shop

In Bennington:

Betty Towne Antiques, 520 South Street, Box 97, Bennington, VT 05201. Tel: (802) 442-9204. Open daily 9-5. Betty Towne. In business for more than thirty years, Betty Towne features small furniture, pressed, art, and cut glass, china, and miscellaneous items. Prices range from $5 to $1,000.

In Brattleboro:

Brooks House Antiques, Brooks House Mall, Brattleboro, VT 05301. Tel: (802) 254-4200. Open Mo-Sa 10:30-5. Norma Chase. Located near the Brattleboro Museum and Art Center, this shop features antique jewelry, glass, porcelain, silver, Orientalia, and oil paintings priced from $15 to $1,500.

Burlington & Shelburne Museum _____

With a population of some 40,000, Burlington is Vermont's largest city and the industrial center of the state. It is the home of the University of Vermont, founded in 1791 by Ira Allen, brother of Ethan, the Revolutionary War hero. There are a number of fine 19th century buildings which testify to the city's prosperity during those years. For collectors, though, Burlington's significance is that it is located only seven miles north of the Shelburne Museum, the finest collection of Americana in the world, and a lesser-known but legitimate rival of Williamsburg.

What to See

Head of Church Street Historic District. Three buildings make up this district in downtown Burlington. The *Unitarian Church*, a Federal-style brick structure built in 1816 from plans by Peter Banner, designer of Boston's Park Street Church, with assistance from Charles Bulfinch. The church has a square, balustraded steeple tower, topped by a porch, octagonal belfry, and lantern. The five-story *Masonic Temple*, a brick Romanesque structure built in 1898, sits on the southwest corner of Church St. Across the street is the *Richardson Building*, now a department store, built in 1896. Eclectic in design, it resembles a French chateau.

University Green Historic District. A central green donated by Ira Allen forms a centerpiece for a number of historically important homes and buildings that fan outward across the University of Vermont campus. Most visible is the *Ira Allen Chapel*, with its 170-foot high tower, built by McKim, Mead, and White in late Georgian style. You'll want to see the *Robert Hull Fleming Museum*, which has a number of important works by Winslow Homer and Albert Bierstadt, as well as an Egyptian mummy and Sitting Bull's scalping equipment. The *Billings Student Center*, built as a library in 1886, was designed by Boston architect H.S. Richardson who considered the Romanesque showpiece his finest work. A bit to the south is *Grassmount*, built for businessman Thadeus Tuttle in 1804. It's a late Georgian brick mansion which now serves as a women's dorm.

The Shelburne Museum, Rte. 7, seven miles south of Burlington. The essential destination in Vermont for fans of great collections, this complex of thirty-five buildings spread across forty-five acres near the shores of Lake Champlain is the most important gathering of folk art, homecrafts, needlework, furnishings, and other types of Americana in the nation. Electra Havemeyer Webb began collecting American folk art in the 1920s and in 1947, she and her husband J. Watson Webb, a rich Vermonter, began developing this extraordinary village. Over the next ten years, they bough a number of old barns, schoolhouses, an inn, a railway depot, even a lighthouse, and moved them here from their original locations throughout New England to house Mrs. Webb's incomparable collections. Although the them in Early American, the structures span three centuries of architectural styles and are filled with treasures that are sure to delight every collector. Among the most interesting sites in this collection of collections:

Hat and Fragrance Unit. An 1800 building from Shelburne village houses the museum's world-renowned collection of American quilts and coverlets dating from the 17th century to the present. Don't miss the "Thirty-Two Birds" applique quilt, from Maryland, c. 1865, and especially the "Princess Feather" applique quilt, c. 1825-1850. Also on display are shell dolls, doll houses, Paris gowns, rugs, samplers, and other needlework.

Dorset House. An 1840 structure houses a collection of more than a thousand hand-carved bird decoys, including geese, ducks, swans, and loons. Among the best are Canada geese decoys carved by Captain Osgood, a Salem, MA ship captain, who carved these splendid examples on trips around the tip of South America to San Francisco during the 1840s. Also, outstanding duck examples by Philadelphia sportsman John Blair, from the 1860s.

Stagecoach Inn. Moved to Shelburne form Charlotte, VT, this 1783 inn was once an inn on the stage route between Canada and southern New England. Today, it houses the museum's outstanding collection of American folk sculpture. Weathervanes and whirligigs, ship figureheads, sternboards, trade signs, cigar store Indians, and eagles. See the four-foot high Columbia weathervane, patented in 1868 by Cushing & White of Waltham, MA and the slightly larger Indian archer weathervane, found in Pennsylvania c. 1810.

Tuckaway General Store. An 1840 brick building which originally stood in nearby Shelburne, this recreation of 19th century life offers displays of every type of general story merchandise of the period, as well as a post office, barbershop, apothecary, a doctor's and dentist's office, complete with the appropriate tools of the trade.

SS Ticonderoga. The museum's one official national historic landmark, this 220-foot side-wheeler plied the waters of Lake Champlain for nearly fifty years hauling freight and passengers. Mrs. Webb saved it from the scrap heap in 1953 and moved it to this site on a specially constructed dike. Photos, ship memorabilia, and a film highlight the ship's colorful past.

Colchester Reef Lighthouse. A handsome Victorian structure formerly located in the waters off Colchester Point in Lake Champlain, this 1871 lighthouse now serves as a gallery in which maritime prints, ship figureheads, and paintings, as well as scrimshaw is shown.

Prentis House. Constructed in Hadley, MA in 1733, this splendid old house is impeccably furnished with antiques and also features displays of 17th and 18th century needlework and delft.

Horseshoe Barn. Built on this site in 1949, this horseshoe-shaped barn is a replica of a barn near Georgia, VT. Some 150 horse-drawn carriages and sleighs are displayed here. The best museum of early transportation to be found anywhere, there are buggies, stage coaches, phaetons, Concord Coaches, even a covered wagon.

Circus Parade Building. A semicircular building, this structure houses a 525-foot model circus parade, carousel horses, and hundreds of circus posters.

Webb Gallery. A new building built to house Mrs. Webb's collection of three hundred years of American painting, ranging from the simple primitive paintings of the colonial period, through Hudson River landscapes of the 19th century, to contemporary artists like Grandma Moses and Andrew Wyeth.

And those are only the highlights. Plan to spend at least a full day exploring the museum. The Shelburne Museum is open from mid-May to late October 9-5 daily; the rest of the year four buildings are open only on Su 11-4. Admission is $5.50 for adults; under fifteen, $2.50.

Where to Stay

See *The Middlebury Inn* under **Middlebury & Brandon.**

Where to Shop

In Burlington:

Designers Circle, 21 Church Street, Burlington, VT 05401. Tel: (802) 864-4238. Open daily 9:30-5:30. Dennis & Judy Bosch, Riki Moss, Charles Dooley. Features handmade pottery, blown glass, pewter, quilts, jewelry, wood, and other crafts. Prices range from $3 to $1,000.

In Shelburne:

Antique Clock and Gun Shop, Village Green, Shelburne, VT 05842. Tel: (802) 985-3000. Open daily, except Su, 11-5. James C. Raymond. Investment quality weapons and time-pieces, with secondary emphasis on furniture, decoys, instruments and other mechanical items. Prices from $100 to $25,000.

Gadhues Antiques, Rte. 7 in the Village, Shelburne, VT 05482. Tel: (802) 985-2682. Open daily 9-5 in summer; by chance in winter. Rene H. and Helen R. Gadhue. Early furniture, glassware, china, textiles, and primitives. In business more than forty-four years.

Manchester & Environs

Manchester has been a favored resort town since the early 1800s. Among the regular visitors to these pastoral parts were Mrs. Abraham Lincoln, whose son Robert lived in nearby Hildene, Mrs. U.S. Grant, Teddy Roosevelt, and William Howard Taft. The center of the village is dominated by a complex of resort buildings known as the Equinox House Historic District. Greek Revivial buildings line both sides of Main and Union streets. Manchester is also a good jumping off point for picturesque southern Vermont villages like Grafton and Danby.

What to See

Hildene, Rte. 7. This splendid Georgian Colonial Revival manor house was built in 1904 and served as the summer home of Robert Todd Lincoln and his family. The Lincoln estate comprised 412 acres and visitors today can enjoy the formal gardens as well as the interior charms of this twenty-four-room mansion. Many of the originals furnishings are on view, including a 1908 Aeolian which presides over the main entrance hall. Open May 23 to October 25, daily 10-4. Admission is $3 for adults; $1 for children aged six to fourteen.

The Museum of American Fly Fishing. Rte. 7. As any good fly fisherman can tell you, Manchester is the home of The Orvis Company, makers of fine fly-fishing equipment since 1856. Exhibits include memorabilia associated with great fishermen, and colorful displays of tackle and equipment.

Where to Stay

Birch Hill Inn, West Road, PO Box 346, Manchester, VT 05254. Tel: (802) 362-2761. Five rooms, three with private baths; one cottage. Rooms run $32 to $53 per person. Reservations should be made two to three months in advance for the fall season; several weeks the rest of the year. Owners: Jim and Pat Lee.

A charming, informal Colonial-style country house perched atop a beautifully landscaped hill, the experience here is like being a guest in someone's country home which, indeed, it is. Guests eat at one large table, "family-style." Breakfast, which is included in the price of accomodations, is usually a hearty affair consisting of eggs, homemade muffins, french toast, and so on. The Lees also cook supper for guests and their friends by reservation. There is a huge living room with an extensive library and some fine paintings. The guest rooms are large and some have restored beams. All have a view out toward the mountains, the pond, or the farm land. Located about five minutes from the heart of Manchester.

Where to Shop

In Danby:

Danby Antiques Center, Main Street, Danby, VT 05739. Tel: (802) 293-9984. Open daily April 1 to November 1, 10-5; November to March, Th-Su 10-5. Agnes and Bill Franks. Specializes in folk art, toys, teddy bears, hooked rugs, early country furniture, and so on. Prices range from $5 to $2,500.

In Grafton:

Gabriel's Barn at Woodchuck Hill Farm Inn, Middletown Road, Grafton, VT 05146. Tel: (802) 843-2398. Open daily 9-5:30. Anne and Frank Gabriel. Among the offerings here are stoneware jugs and crocks, primitives, kitchen ware, tools, country furniture, pewter, brass, and copper. Prices from $5 to $2500.

In Manchester:

Paraphernalia Antiques, Rte. 7 South, Manchester, VT 05254. Tel: (802) 362-2421. Open daily 10-5:30. Anne Alenick. In business over twenty-five years, this shop sells jewelry, silver, miniatures, bronzes, sewing equipment, and enamels priced from $25 to $2,000.

Middlebury & Brandon _____

Middlebury—home of Middlebury College, the oldest community-founded college in America (1800)—is one of the most carefully preserved towns in New England. The fames college campus, with its ivy-covered buildings of gray limestone, blends harmoniously with the many 19th century structures of the town itself. Church spires, tree-lined streets, the sophistication of a college town mixed with the traditional Yankee values, all add us to a pleasant experience for the visitor. A few miles to the south, Brandon has two of the finest village greens in the Northeast and several fine antique shops.

What to See

Middlebury Village Historic District. Some 275 buildings are included within this district which radiates out from the village green and Courthouse Square to include Main and several other small street. Of these, 57 are said to have "outstanding historical or architectural significance. Among them is the "Congregational Church," built on Main Street between 1806 and 1809, by Lavius Fillmore. A magnificent structure, which dominates the heart of the city, Fillmore's masterpiece is marked by an unusual steeple: a spire and two octagonal stages on top of three detailed and textured tiers. The *David Nichols House*, 28 Weybridge Street, is considered the finest example of Greek Revival architecture in Middlebury, no mean feat considering the extraordinary number of such houses here.

Sheldon Art Museum, Archaeological and Historical Society, 1 Park Street. Built by Eben Judd, founder of the marble industry in Middlebury, in 1829, this elegant blend of Federal and Greek Revival styles is an impressive seventeen-room mansion. Henry Sheldon bought the house in 1882, hung out a sign that read "Sheldon Art Museum, Archaeological and Historical Society," thus establishing the first incorporated village museum in the United States. The heart of the museum's collection consists of 19th century household furnishings--clocks, pianos, portraits, books, china, and assorted bric-a-brac. A country store on the grounds sells "old-timey" items. One hour guided tours are conducted Mo-Sa 10-5 between June 1 and October 15. Admission, including the tour, is $2.

Morgan Horse Farm. If you fancy horses, you won't want to miss the University of Vermont's Morgan Horse Farm, two-and-one-half miles north of Middlebury. A Woodstock singing teacher named Justin Morgan received a colt as payment for a debt in the 1780s. Although the horse--whose name was Figure--stood only fourteen hands high, he was stronger than most logging horses and could outrun thoroughbreds. Aware that he was on to something important, Morgan began breeding the horse and thus established the first native American breed. Colonel Joseph Battell—publisher of the Middlebury *Register*—built this lush, 100-acre farm in the late 1800s, compiled a Morgan registry, and made the Morgan an official, legitimate breed. Guided tours, including an 1878 barn, are conducted daily 10-4 between May and October. Admission is $1.75.

Where to Stay

The Middlebury Inn, 17 Pleasant Street, Middlebury, VT 05753. Tel: In Vermont (802) 388-4961; Out-of-State (800) 842-4666. Seventy-seven rooms, sixty-three with private baths. Doubles, with bath, run $56 to $80. Space is usually available for walk-ins, but reservatons are suggested. Innkeepers: Frank and Jane Emanuel.

This historic inn, in business since 1827, is located in the heart of Middlebury. The Main House, a stately three-story brick structure, has welcomed thousands of weary travelers

since. Each wing of the building has a different personality.
There are wide hallways, high ceilings, nooks and sitting
areas, and pleasant, unexpected surprises like hand-cut
lampshades, small libraries, spool beds, and papered sprinkler
pipes. On the first floor, there is a warm and spacious lobby
with cozy nooks for reading. The Morgan Room Tavern is a
favorite watering hole and the wedgwood colored main dining
room is a return to old-time elegance. Open seven days a week
for breakfast, lunch, and dinner, it features traditional New
England fare. Located close to everything.

Where to Shop

In Brandon:

H. Cray Gildersleeve Antiques, 57 Park Street, Brandon,
VT 05733. Tel: (802) 247-6684. Open 10-5, or by appointment. H. Cray Gildersleeve. Specializes in folk art, early iron,
and woodcarving. Prices $20 and up.

Stoney Fields Antiques, Inc., RD 2, Brandon, VT 05733.
Tel: (802) 247-6711. Open daily 10-5 between June 1 and
October 15; by appointment the rest of the year. Walter Cerf
and William Dutton. In business more than twenty years, the
specialties here are American, English, Continental, and Oriental works of art, formal, country and primitive furniture,
porcelains, silver, ivory, and rugs. Prices range from $20 to
$30,000.

In Middlebury:

Benjamin Fig, 61 Main Street, Middlebury, VT 05753.
Tel: (802) 388-2212. Open Mo-Sa 9-5. Philip and Sharon
Coleman. Handwrought silver and gold jewelry, tin ware,
handmade crockery, unique playing cards, stone reproductions
of Early American and architectural reliefs. Prices from $5 to
$250.

Bix Antiques, Rte. 116, Case Street, Middlebury, VT
05753. Tel: (802) 388-2277. Open Mo-Sa 8-5. John Wetmore.
A constantly changing line of collectibles, furniture, folk art,
tin, lamps, and so on, ranging from $5 to $2,000 and up.

Carob Leather/Carob Creek Wools, 4 Park Street,
Middlebury, VT 05753. Open daily 10-5. Janet Higbee and
Dorothy Walsh. Specializes in leather goods, from small acces-
sories to garments; handmade sweaters.

Copper Kettle Antiques, 74 Main Street, Middlebury, VT 05753. Tel: (802) 388-7545. Open Mo-Sa 9:30-5. S.H. Conn, Jr. Offers a general line, but specializes in antique American and English copper and brass. Prices range up to $1,000.

Hobnob Antiques, Rte. 7 South, Middlebury, VT 05753. Tel: (802) 388-6813. Open daily 11-6. Elizabeth and Robert Templeton. The Templetons feature refinished antique furniture, blue decorated stoneware, prints, and Early American pattern glass. Prices from $5 to $1,500.

Vermont State Craft Center at Frog Hollow, Middlebury, VT 05753. Tel: (802) 388-3177. Open Mo-Sa 9:30-5. Ann Roth. The nation's first craft center, visitors can watch Vermont artisans working in this old factory building. A shop displays and sells the works of more than two hundred and fifty craftsmen in pottery, pewter, wood, metals, fibers, and glass. Eight special exhibits each year. Prices range from $1.50 to $4,000.

The Village Store of Middlebury, Rte. 7 South, Middlebury, VT 05753. Tel: (802) 388-6476. Open Mo-Sa 9-5. Jean and Ted Panicucci. Features 18th and 19th century furniture, primitives, and accessories. Prices from $2 to $5,000.

Montpelier, Barre, & Stowe

These three east central Vermont towns all have plenty of charm for the unhurried traveler. Montpelier, the state capital since 1805, is nestled among the wooden hillsides above the Winooski River. Barre is home to the largest granite quarry in the world. Stowe is one of the leading ski centers of the East Coast. The combination is a little off-beat, but distinctly worth a visit.

What to See

Montpelier Historic District, State Street and Main Street. The main attraction here is the *Vermont State House*, whose gleaming gold-leaf dome is visible for miles. Constructed of granite and decorated with marble, this Greek Revival masterpiece was built between 1833 and 1838, then extensively renovated in 1859. The downtown area has burned to the ground a number of times in the past so the State House is one of the few structures in the area that date beyond the 1870s. Just down the street is the *Pavilion Office Building*, a reconstruction of the 1875 Pavilion Hotel which stood on the site until 1971. It's a charming example of Steamboat Gothic architecture and home to the Vermont Historical Society. Nearby, on Main Street is the *Wood Art Gallery*, housed in the Kellogg-Hubbard Library. It has more than a hundred works by Thomas Waterman Wood, a Montpelier painter of the romantic scene genre, who died in 1903, as well as other American painters of the same school. Wood's home and studio, called *Athenwood*, at 41 and 49 Northfield Street, are charming Gothic Revival structures. Although privately-owned, they can be viewed from the street.

Rock of Ages Quarry, Barre. For nearly a hundred and fifty year, Barre has set the standard for high quality granite and dozens of quarries have operated here. The four still active are run by the Rock of Ages Company, noted for its memorials and tombstones. Guided tours are conducted by the company from May through October 8:30-5. From the edge of the quarry, there's a 350-foot view down to the bottom of the mine where enormous stone-moving equipment is working away. Visitors may also tour a Craftsman Center in the nearby factory where the stones are finished and polished.

Trapp Family Lodge, Stowe. Skiing is Stowe's big attraction, but "Sound of Music" fans won't want to miss this Tyrolian chalet built by the famed Austrian family here because the site reminded them of their native country. Open year-round.

Where to Shop

In Barre:

Arnholm's Antiques, 891 North Main Street, Barre, VT 05641. Tel: (802) 476-5921. Open year-round, by appointment only. Rachel Arnholm. In business for more than forty years, Arnholm's specializes in antique and estate jewelry (all gold pieces).

In East Barre:

Farr's Antiques, Rte. 110, East Barre, VT 05649. Tel: (802) 476-4308. Open 10-4 year-round. Antiques of all kinds, Victorian and country furniture, glass, china, clocks, and old tools. Prices from $15 to $2,500.

Larson's Clock Shop, Upper Waterman Road, East Barre, VT 05641. Tel: (802) 476-7524. Open daily, year-round. Lindy Larson. Larson's specializes in antique clocks of all types and also does clock restoration.

In East Montpelier:

Jeffrey R. Cueto Antiques, Murray Road, East Montpelier, VT 05651. Tel: (802) 223-5175. Open by appointment only. American furniture and accessories. Prices range from $20 to $2,000 and up.

In Montpelier:

Conversation Piece, 121 Barre Street, Montpelier, VT 05602. Tel: (802) 223-7774. Open We-Sa 10-4. Lindsay Wade. Features antique furniture, vintage clothing, and "good old stuff." Prices from 25¢ to $1,200.

Weaver's Web, 23 Langdon Street, Montpelier, VT 05602. Tel: (802) 229-5803. Open 9:30-5:30 Mo-Th; 9:30-8:00 Fr; 9:30-5:00 Sa. Judy Chase. Knitting, weaving, and craft supplies and yarns, $2 to $25. Looms from $100 to $1,000.

Doll People, 121 Barre Street, Montpelier, VT 05602. Tel: (802) 223-6976. Open Mo-Sa 10-4. Joann McCracken. Handmade dolls, miniature, and porcelain.

Mureta's Antiques, 24 State Street, Montpelier, VT 05602. Tel: (802) 229-4476. Open daily 10-5. Gary Mureta. Features a general line, including baskets, Victorian and primitive furniture, prints, china, glass, rugs, quilts, silver, lamps, and so on. Prices range from $1 to $1,000.

Stephen Jones Antiques, Hill St, Montpelier, VT 05602. Tel: (802) 223-6844. Open daily. Offers a wide range of country antiques including a large selection of paper items. Prices from $5 to $500.

In Stowe:

Green Mountain Antiques of Stowe, Main Street, Stowe, VT 05672. Tel: (802) 253-4369. Open 11-5 all year round. Russell and Judy Foregger. Selected furniture, primitives, quilts, silver, miniature and decorative accessories. Prices from $2.50 to $5,000.

The Stowe Pottery and Craft Gallery, Rte. 108, Stowe, VT 05672. Tel: (802) 253-4693. Open daily 9-5. Jean-Paul

Patnode. Features paperweights, handmade marbles, and so on. Prices from $3 to $300.

Woodstock

To stroll along Elm and Pleasant Streets and browse in the shop windows that line Central Street is to step back into the 18th and 19th centuries in this, the most handsome of all Vermont villages. Woodstock has been blessed by wealth and an absence of industry, mixed with residents who value the past. The result is a gracious town that has remained basically unchanged over the years. Be sure to check the Town Crier bulletin board near the corner of Elm and Central Streets for notices of flea markets, bazaars, and other village events.

What to See

Woodstock Historical Society, 26 Elm Street. Constructed in 1807, this handsome frame and brick Federal mansion was built by merchant Charles Dana and was occupied by his descendants until 1944. The focus here is on the decorative arts from the period 1800 to 1860—clocks, dolls, clothing, silver, and textiles. An adjacent barn houses a display of farm and household tools. Guided tours are conducted Mo-Sa 9-5 from Memorial Day through October; Su, 10-2. Admission: $1.50.

Norman Williams Library. Dr. Williams, a longtime Woodstock physician, endowed this 50,000-volume library. Even more impressive is the collection of Japanese arts and crafts that he commissioned on a visit to Japan in the 1880s. Silver sake bowls, Satsuma ware, lacquers, household items of previous metals and bronze highlight this distinguished collection. Open Mo-Sa 9-5. Free.

Ottauquechee D.A.R. House, on The Green. Built in 1807, this seven-room mansion houses exhibits ranging from Revolutionary War artifacts to furniture and household furnishings. Also on display is a Hiram Powers marble bust titled *America*, personified by a woman with one breast uncovered. It was intended for the White House but President Franklin Pierce turned it down. Railroad memorabilia from the ill-fated Woodstock Railroad include a train bell and conductor's lantern. Open Mo-Sa 2-4 during July and August.

Where to Stay

Woodstock Inn and Resort, 14 The Green, Woodstock, VT 05091. Tel: (802) 457-1100. One hundred and twenty rooms, all with baths. Rooms run $78 to $125; suites to $275. Reservations should be made up to twelve months in advance. General manager: Chet Williamson.

Not the original and not cheap, this is still the place to stay in Woodstock. Located a mere 206 feet from The Green, the Colonial-style Inn is surrounded by landscaped gardens and native trees. It has three stories in front and four stories on the garden side. Guest rooms are decorated with specially designed furniture and colorful handmade bed quilts. Walls are decorated with prints from the local photography school. The handsome lobby has several paintings, including many of early Woodstock by one of the owners of the original Inn which was torn down and replaced by this version in 1969. The Inn is owned by Laurance Rockefeller who spent $3 million to bury all the telephone poles around The Village Green. Where else in the world can you sit on a broad terrace in a rocking chair and listen to no less than four Paul Revere bells chiming evensong? There's a coffee shop and a nicely decorated main dining room which features a lavish Saturday evening buffet and a gala Sunday brunch.

Index